I0475560

PROFITABLE STOCK OPTIONS TRADING

A Beginner's Guide

Lessons I Learned Losing $100,000

To Accelerate Your Trading Success

Ged Cusack

First published in the US in 2017

Copyright © Ged Cusack, 2017

The moral right of the author has been asserted.

All rights reserved.

No part of this publication may be reproduced, stored in a retrieval system, or transmitted, in any form or by any means, without the prior permission in writing of the author, nor be otherwise circulated in any form of binding or cover other than that in which it is published and without a similar condition including this condition being imposed on the subsequent purchaser.

ISBN 978-1-544-27082-1

DISCLAIMER

This publication is designed to provide competent and reliable information regarding the subject matter covered. However, it is sold with the understanding that the author and the publisher are not engaged in rendering legal, financial or other professional advice. Laws and practices often vary from state to state and country to country and if legal or expert assistance is required, the services of a professional should be sought. The author and publisher specifically disclaim any liability that is incurred from the use or application of the contents of this book.

The publisher does not have any control over and does not assume any responsibility for authors of third party websites and their content.

This book is dedicated to my ex-wife, Rata.

During my initial trading and the subsequent losses she was there to provide positive encouragement and support.

She was never judgemental and constantly affirmed that I was capable of succeeding.

I absorbed her enthusiasm and attribute my quest to support others partly to her.

A huge thank you to Carlos and Oli for their mentorship. My eternal gratitude to my fellow traders Gee and Murray for their continued support throughout my trading journey.

Extra thanks go out to my amazing friend and editor Jennifer Manson.

Thank you Dean for the invaluable proofreading.

CONTENTS

INTRODUCTION

"Rule No.1: Never lose money. Rule No.2: Never forget Rule No.1."
– Warren Buffett

Warren Buffett is arguably one of the most successful traders of all time and he is so successful because he has consistently traded profitably year on year.

It might seem obvious that you don't want to lose money trading but it has to be acknowledged from the outset that statistically you will have some losing trades.

If your risk profile/psychology cannot cope with the fact that you will take some losses perhaps trading is not for you.

The odds state that 90-97% (depending on which source you accept) of day traders lose money.

Reading some trading books, blogs and other publications, a lot of traders only focus on their profits. Successful traders know that some losses are inevitable and for you to succeed it's important that you accept that fact.

The intention of this book is not to say to you that you have no chance of being a successful trader.

In Scott Adams' fantastic book "How to Fail at Almost Everything and Still Win Big" he talks about his experiences and failures in order to benefit others.

"If losers gave seminars I'd attend and take good notes."
– Jim Rohn

It is in the spirit of Scott and mentors such as Jim Rohn I offer you this book so that you can benefit from my losses and learnings.

Some individuals (Schadenfreudes) actually feel better when they see others who are not doing as well as themselves. Although it wasn't my intention when writing this book to feed those egos, if that's one of the things that gets you through the day I offer this as an extra benefit.

They say that you never truly understand anything until you can explain it to an eight-year-old, and although some of the concepts and maths in this book may be above the level of an eight-year-old, I have tried to make the information accessible to all.

The purpose of this book is to educate you. I want you to be the best informed trader possible so that you can succeed.

This is not intended as a book that will automatically take you from $10,000 to a million dollars in one fell swoop.

I've included details of even my smallest learnings as when you first start out you don't know what you don't know.

The trading world (despite what some may say) is not a case of one size fits all.

There are some good books out there that chronicle a diary of someone's trading (e.g. "Making Money from CFD trading" by Catherine Davey).

I accumulated my ($100,000) losses over a period of approximately four years. I believe that padding out this book with a journal of four years of trading logs will not benefit you.

Rather than just give you a bunch of trades to dissect I have focused on the important learnings to maximize the benefits to you. I have detailed some of my larger trades, such as my ZFX trade in chapter two (where I lost over $10,000).

During my initial trading journey there were some difficult times (including the breakup of my marriage). As I am a firm believer in getting to the crux of the info I have attempted to make this book as frank as possible, whilst providing as many useful kernels of information for you as I can.

It's intended that this warts and all book will provide something for all levels of traders.

My trading journey

I first became aware of Options Trading from a friend who had attended an Anthony Robbins weekend. Robert Kiyosaki mentions Options in some of his *Rich Dad* books but it was a friend's recommendation that set me on the Options path.

Fate determined that a couple of years after that recommendation I was next exposed to Options.

Having just completed 22 years in the British military I had moved to New Zealand (NZ) with my kiwi wife and was looking for a new venture to pursue.

I was glancing through the paper one day and I saw an article about an Australian trading mentor who had just visited Christchurch, the New Zealand city I was living in. Unfortunately I had just missed his intro evening.

I noted that he was soon to run a three day course in another New Zealand city so I contacted his company.

The course was about $4,000 at the time and as I could afford to invest that much I jumped in feet first.

When I booked the course I actually had to ask them to recommend a hotel as I had only been in New Zealand a couple of months and the course was at the other end of the country.

I did start the course with little due diligence but I have no regrets looking back.

I believe that when you go into a venture, as long as you learn from any setbacks, those snags (financial or otherwise) are just classed as training costs.

I have provided further information on my training in the chapter on *Training & Mentors*.

Although I took a trading hiatus for about 24 months I came back to trading with a new-found vigour in 2011.

The layout of this book and how to use it

Although this book is not designed to be a stand-alone course in trading I am assuming that the readers will be at various levels and as such I have tried to provide enough insight to make it accessible to all.

If you are brand new to Options trading (or are primarily looking at Options as insurance for your stock portfolio) I suggest that you read section one of the book first. This section is designed to provide you with a solid foundation – so if skipping section one results in some bad trading decisions you can add that to your own learnings.

Section One

Because I wanted this to be an inclusive book, the first section of the book is designed as a foundation to Options trading.

Understanding Calls and Puts is a foundation to Options trading. The book begins with explanations of the basics of these Options, candlesticks and other charting.

I have also provided insights into the liquidity of markets and trends/market direction trading. Just understanding the definition of an Option is not enough to enter the trading arena so this part of the book gives you a better feel for the markets.

Although it may not seem a basic subject to some, the chapter on Options as insurance (*How to use Options to insure your stock portfolio*) is also included in this first section. Some individuals may just want to use Stock Options as insurance rather than trade them in a more active mode so this is an important foundation chapter for them.

Section Two

The second section of this book is about getting established as a trader.

Psychology is one of the most important factors in trading so I have covered this here first.

I have talked about my training and mentors as learning from books can only take you so far on your trading journey. As a trading library is a must for all traders I have also included a recommended reading list at the rear of the book.

Individuals tend to underestimate the initial time requirements of trading so I suggest that you read the chapter on time commitments prior to the business plan chapter.

Creating your business plan, trading rules and maintaining good money management processes are all equally important so I encourage you to read all of these chapters together.

I have also provided an overview of advanced Options trading strategies. As I want you to have an established foundation first, these strategies are at the rear of this section. Don't look at these strategies unless you are sure that you have a firm grasp on the previous chapters.

Summary

Dependent on your current level of trading you can read this book from start to finish or just dip into the relevant sections that you feel are useful.

I know there are traders out there with varying levels of experience, but as some of my errors are common trading mistakes, I hope that the chapters serve as a reminder to the experienced trader not to go down this road (or not to retrace their previous steps down this road).

If you are like me, you like condensed information, so at the rear of this book is a consolidated list of the book's learnings.

My aim is to provide honesty and insight into the mistakes I made along the way and my wish for you is that this book contributes to your future success.

NB: Although the figures in this book vary from American, Australian & New Zealand dollars, wherever you are going to trade you can substitute your own currencies.

Top Tips

Although the book is full of learnings, in the spirit of being concise I have listed below what I think are six of the most important tips for trading.

My 6 Top Trading Tips

1. Know yourself well before you risk money trading (psychology is an essential key for every successful trader).
2. Practice good money management techniques (of the 90% + traders who fail in the market, a high percentage fail because they run out of money).
3. Choose your mentors or instructors carefully (your psychology and risk profile may not be compatible for you to adopt their systems).
4. Have a set of Trading Rules and stick to them (you don't necessarily need as many as I have in Chapter 10).
5. Understand the time commitments and how much time you will require to learn to trade successfully (trading is an art, a skill and a profession).
6. To be a successful trader you need to consistently make profits (a few good trades are not enough).

SECTION ONE

Chapter 1   Basic Call & Put Options explained

In the dictionary the term Option can be defined as "a choice" or "an opportunity".

Whenever people refer to an Option in the financial markets it is actually an abbreviation of "an Options contract". You need to be aware that in the world of finance an Option is a legally binding contract.

The term Option refers to the ability to purchase or sell a financial asset (e.g. a number of shares) but not the obligation to purchase or sell that financial asset.

There are certain restrictions on that contract and these are: the price that you can purchase or sell that asset for (known as the strike price); and the deadline for which the contract remains extant (the expiry date).

This means that even though you have a contract to buy or sell, you have the Option (choice) to purchase or sell only if completion of that transaction benefits you.

There is a vast variation of Options trading strategies available but as the basic Call and Put Options provide their basis in one combination or another I'll focus on them first.

Call Options

Purchasing a Call Option on a stock gives the buyer the Option (but not the obligation) to purchase a set quantity of a stock at a set price until a set date.

E.g. If you bought an ABC $10.00 Dec 24th Call Option, the contract allows you the Option to buy a set number of ABC shares (In America one contract usually refers to 100 shares) at $10.00 a share until Dec 24th.

Why you would purchase a Call Option

If you believed that a stock was going to go up in value, but did not want to risk the full purchase price of the stock, a Call Option gives you leverage. You can tie in the price that you want to pay for a stock (for a fee) without risking the whole purchase price of that stock.

Once the stock goes up you can buy the stock at the lower price stated on your Call Option and then sell the stock at the new higher market price.

The legally binding Options contract means that whoever sold you the Call Option has to sell you the stock at that lower price.

NB: In reality most Options traders would just sell the Option at its new higher value rather than own the stock (see intrinsic value further in this chapter).

Put Options

Purchasing a Put Option on a stock gives the buyer the Option (but not the obligation) to sell a set quantity of that stock at a set price until a set date.

E.g. If you bought an XYZ $10.00 Dec 24th Put Option, the contract allows you the Option to sell a set number of XYZ shares (In America one contract usually refers to 100 shares) at $10.00 a share until Dec 24th.

Why you would purchase a Put Option

If you believed that a stock was going to go down in value and wanted to profit from this price move you could buy a Put Option on that stock.

Once the stock goes down you can buy the stock at the new lower market price and then sell the same stock at the earlier higher price stated on your Put Option.

Another reason for you to purchase a Put Option is if you wanted to insure your current stock holding from a fall in the stock's price (we will cover this in the chapter on *How to use Options to insure your stock portfolio*).

The legally binding Options contract means that whoever sold you the Put Option has to purchase that stock from you at that higher price.

NB: In reality, unless an Options trader already owns the stock, most Options traders would just sell the Option at its new higher value rather than trade the stock (see intrinsic value further in this chapter).

Options in layman's terms

I believe that the analogy of a house purchase can provide a simplified explanation of how Options work, so I have provided a couple of examples below to demonstrate this premise.

For simplicity, in the two case studies below, the Options contracts only refer to one house (whereas a stock Option contract can usually cover 100 or more shares).

NB: The cash values below are only for simplification but the same concept will obviously apply for different quantities and prices.

Case Study 1: Buying a Call Option on a house

We see a house that is currently selling for $100,000.

We can't afford to pay $100,000 this month but we think that the house will go up in price so we approach the vendor with a Contract (proposal).

Our contract states that we will pay the Vendor $1,000 for the Option (the right but not the obligation) to purchase the house at the list price of $100,000.

The contract is valid for 30 days and if we don't purchase the house within that time period the vendor will keep the $1,000 and there is no further commitment on either of our behalf.

We have in fact purchased the equivalent of a one month Call Option on the property.

Exercising the Option or not

You make the choice whether or not you exercise an Option or let it expire worthless (depending on which gives you the most financial benefit).

When we talk about exercising a contract we are actually referring to putting into effect the rights that were specified in that contract (i.e. implementing the purchase or sale at a set price within the set time frame).

When we decide to exercise the contract

If the housing market soars (in the next 30 days) and the house is now valued at $110,000 we can exercise our Call Option and buy the house for $100,000.

What does that mean for us in financial terms?

$110,000 (Current House Market Value) − $1,000 (Our Option Price) − $100,000 (Previous House Purchase Price) = $9,000 (Our Savings).

By purchasing the Call Option and exercising it, although we spent $1,000 on the Option we have still purchased the house for $9,000 less than its current market value.

When we decide to let the contract expire

If the housing market crashes (in the next 30 days) and the house is now valued at $90,000) we let our Option expire worthless and buy the house for the market value of $90,000.

We had the right to buy at $100,000 but not the contractual obligation.

What does that mean for us in financial terms?

$100,000 (The House's Initial House Value) – $1,000 (Our Option Price) – $90,000 (New House Purchase Price) = $9,000 (Our Savings).

By purchasing the Call Option but letting the contract expire worthless, although we spent $1,000 on the Option we have still purchased the house for $9,000 less than we would have paid a month ago.

NB: There could be various fees incurred on the transaction but these basic numbers are just to explain the concept to you.

LEARNING 1.1 – If an underlying asset has a market value less than the strike price of your Call Option (at expiry) there is no point exercising that Call Option.

Case Study 2: Buying a Put Option on a house

We have a house that we are currently selling for $100,000.

We think that the house prices may fall but don't want to sell the house this month. We approach a purchaser with a Contract (proposal).

Our contract states that we will pay the purchaser $1,000 for the Option (the right but not the obligation) to sell the house at the list price of $100,000.

The contract is valid for 30 days and if we don't sell the house within that time period the purchaser will keep the $1,000 and there is no further commitment on either of our behalf.

We have in fact purchased the equivalent of a one month Put Option on the property.

Exercising the Option or not

You make the choice whether or not you exercise an Option or let it expire worthless (depending on which gives you the most financial benefit).

When we talk about exercising a contract we are actually referring to putting into effect the rights that were specified in that contract (i.e. implementing the purchase or sale at a set price within the set time frame).

When we decide to let the contract expire
If the housing market soars (in the next 30 days) and the house is now valued at $110,000 we let our Option expire worthless and we can sell the house at the market value of $110,000.

We had the right to sell at $100,000 but not the contractual obligation.

What does that mean for us in financial terms?

$110,000 (The House Current Market Value) − $1,000 (Option Price) - $100,000 (Initial House List Price) = $9,000 (Our Profits).

By purchasing the Put Option but letting the contract expire worthless, although we spent $1,000 on the Option, we have still sold the house for $9,000 more than we would have received a month ago.

NB: There could be various fees incurred on the transaction but these basic numbers are just to explain the concept to you.

When we decide to exercise the contract
If the housing market crashes (in the next 30 days) and the house is now valued at $90,000 we can exercise our Option and sell the house for $100,000.

What does that mean for us in financial terms?

$100,000 (House Sale Price) − $1,000 (Option Price) - $90,000 (The House Current Market Value) = $9,000 (Our locked in value).

By purchasing the Put Option and exercising it, although we spent $1,000 on the Option, we have still sold the house for $9,000 more than its current market value.

NB: On the New York Stock Exchange, a standard Call or Put contract usually covers one hundred underlying shares.

LEARNING 1.2 – If an underlying asset has a market value more than the strike price of your Put Option (at expiry) there is no point exercising that Put Option.

Intrinsic and Time Value

The price value of an Option is determined primarily by a combination of two factors - its intrinsic value and its time value.

Remember that the restrictions on an Options contract are the price that you can purchase or sell that asset for and the timeframe for which the contract remains extant.

The term "Market Maker" refers to the individuals that create the market to allow Options to be traded. These individuals are usually financial institutions. As there would be no trading without someone willing to undertake the opposite side of a contract, Market Makers are integral to the pricing of Options.

The Intrinsic Value

The intrinsic value of an Option relates closely to the price value of the underlying asset that the Option relates to (e.g. stock or commodity etc).

Let's look at a case study to clarify this intrinsic value.

Case Study relating only to Intrinsic Value

- We purchase one contract of a 3 month Call Option on stock XYZ.
- The current stock price is $10.00 per share and the Option's price is $0.50 per share.
- The contract covers 100 Shares so the cost of the Options contract to us is $50 (100 x $0.50).

Overnight the stock price of XYZ rises to $11.00 per share

- The stock has just gone up $1.00 per share and as your contract covers 100 shares the intrinsic value of your Option has just gone up approximately $100.
- So you purchased the contract for $50 and it has now gone up $100 overnight so it is now worth $150 (+200% in one day).

NB: Although intrinsic value isn't exactly on a one to one scale (e.g. in this case a $1 move in a stock price related exactly to a $1 move for each share covered by the Option) it is close enough to show that intrinsic value can have a big effect on the Option value.

Because I initially traded stocks on the Australian Stock Exchange (and some of the stocks such as BHP continued to trade on other markets overnight) there were times when my stock Options had gone up substantially in value overnight.

LEARNING 1.3 – If an underlying asset has a rapid price move, the intrinsic value of the Option can be affected exponentially and rapid action can result in fast profits.

The Time Value

When we referred to purchasing a Call Option on a stock we said it gave the buyer the Option (but not the obligation) to purchase a set quantity of a stock at a set price until a set date.

The set date that the purchase of the asset must be completed by (or the Option is worthless) is called the expiry date.

Option timeframes tend to be referred to in months so if you purchased an Option in mid-January that had an expiry date of April 23rd that would be referred to as a three month Option (as you have approximately three months before its expiry date).

The time value of an Option is a value that is formulated by the market makers and relates to the difference between when the Option is purchased and the date when the Option is due to expire.

The longer the time before expiry the greater the chance that the price of the underlying asset will change and the greater the risk to the person selling the Option. Hence the time value of an Option is really the risk value.

Let's look at a case study to clarify this time value.

Case Study relating only to Time Value

- We purchase one contract of a 3 month Call Option for stock ABC.
- The current stock price is $10.00 per share and the Option's price is $0.65 per share.
- The contract covers 100 Shares so the cost of the Options contract to us is $65 (100 x $0.65).

In just over two months ABC stock is still trading at $10.00 per share

- Because the stock price has remained the same there is no change in the intrinsic value of the Option.

- As the time to expiry has drastically diminished (and thus the risk) the time value of the Option is now only $0.35 per share.
- The contract covers 100 Shares so the value of the Options contract to us is now only $35 (100 x $0.35)
- Although the loss of $30 may not seem a big deal remember that these numbers are just for simplification of the concept. In real terms you have just lost 46% of your stake in this trade.

NB: The time value of an Option tends to diminish a lot faster in the last 10 to 21 days before the Option's expiry date.

I have to admit that early on I did commit the cardinal sin of letting my bought Options expire worthless (on numerous occasions).

LEARNING 1.4 – If an underlying asset has a limited price move over a set period, the Option will still lose value due to time decay, so set a maximum date for holding purchased Options.

American and European Options

Most Options traders will only buy and sell the Option and rarely exercise the Option for the underlying asset.

To be fully informed it is worth you knowing the difference between an American and European Stock Option. It should be noted that most Options traded are American style.

The basic difference is that American Options can be exercised any time up to (and including) the expiration date of the Option whereas the European Options can only be exercised on the date of expiration.

You should be aware that there are some specific deadlines for exercising Options (and dates that you must notify your broker that you wish to exercise them). The main points to note are: what kind of Options you are trading; and are there any idiosyncrasies of that specific Option before you trade it.

Although a lot of individuals trade online nowadays, you should still be able to find out this information from your broker.

If an online broker doesn't have this information readily available, find another broker (or at least wait for the information before proceeding with your trade).

Chapter 2   How to use Options to Insure Your Stock Portfolio

Whichever of the world's stock markets you are using to trade your stocks, there is the potential to use stock Options as an insurance platform for your stock portfolio.

You can only use Options to insure Optionable stocks but a lot of the major stocks in the world are Optionable.

An Optionable stock is a stock that has associated Options available to trade on the relevant exchange.

Insuring with Put Options

The two main forms of basic Options are Puts and Calls. For the purpose of this insurance strategy we shall focus on Puts as they lend themselves to insuring stocks.

The definition of a Put is an Options contract that gives the holder the right to sell a certain quantity of an underlying asset to the writer of the Option, at a specified price (known as the strike price) up to a specified date (known as the expiration date).

In the USA an Options contract usually covers a parcel of 100 shares, in Australia it used to cover a parcel of 1000 shares (but this has been reduced to 100 shares recently).

Because a Put contractually locks in the price at which you can sell your parcel of shares, it can act as an insurance policy.

If your stock portfolio is a safety net for your twilight years the last thing you need is your life savings being decimated by a market crash.

The price you pay for your Put Option will vary dependent on the difference between the strike price (the price that your Put Options contract allows you to sell the stock at) and the market price of the stock when you purchase your Option.

If the price of the stock and the strike price of the Option are the same (when you purchase an Option) the cost you pay for that Option will be primarily time value and only a fractional amount of intrinsic value (see the previous chapter on intrinsic and time value).

Just like most insurances, the cost of this premium (your Put Options) is dependent on how much risk you want to incur. If you insure your stock at a lower strike price than the market value then the difference in those prices is similar to your excess/deductibles for an auto insurance policy. By choosing different strike prices you determine how much of your share's current value to lock in.

Below are two case studies to provide a comparison of purchasing your Puts at different strike prices. The first case relates to a Put with the same strike price as the market price of the underlying stock. The second case relates to a Put at a different strike price than the market price of the same stock.

Case Study 1

You own 1,000 shares of a stock ABC which is currently sitting at a market price of $10 per share.

You decide to buy a Put Option at a strike price of $10.00 with a two month expiry date from today (meaning that you will have the Option to sell the stock at $10.00 a share). Because the standard contract on the New York stock exchange only covers 100 shares you purchase 10 contracts at $100 a contract.

Your Options contracts cost you $1,000 + Brokerage (This is the equivalent of an insurance premium).

In the next month the stock price falls to $8.00 a share.

Your 1,000 ABC shares are now worth only $8,000 but your Put Option allows you to sell the stock for $10,000.

The next step is up to you, whether you exercise the Put Option and sell the shares at $10,000 or you sell the Put Option and keep the shares.

Selling the shares

I'm assuming that as you are astute enough to insure your stocks that you have a view on the direction of the markets. If you believe that the stock is going to fall further you are probably better off selling the stock at your locked in price. Because your price is locked in until the expiry date there is no rush to sell the shares but the sooner you take the reduced capital out of this trade the sooner you can invest it in a more profitable trade.

You sell the shares at $10,000 (the Option's strike price) – $1,000 (the cost of your Options) so your losses on your investment are limited to $1,000.

If you hadn't purchased your insurance you would now be selling your stock for $8,000 (the current market value) and taking a loss of $2,000 (the difference between your stock's previous value and the current price).

By insuring your stock you have reduced your losses by $1,000 (or 10% of your stock's value).

Selling the Put Options

If your view of your stock is that the recent fall in price was a glitch, assuming that you expect that the price will recover very soon, you may want to keep the stock and benefit from the increase in the (intrinsic) value of your Option.

By selling the Put Options you will no longer have any insurance on your stock but for this example we will assume that you have made that choice.

Because the stock has fallen, the value of the Options is now $2,100 (primarily due to the increase in intrinsic value).

By selling the Options at their current value the difference between the relative values are $10,000 (the previous stock price) - $8,000 (the new stock value) + $2,100 (the current value of the Options) - $1,000 (your purchase price of the Options) = $1,100.

So your potential loss is ($2,000-$1,100) $900 instead of the $2,000 potential loss (from the fall in the stock price).

If you are right and the stock goes back up to $10 a share your stock is now worth the original $10,000 but you have gained on the Options trade as you bought the Options for $1,000 and sold them for $2,100.

$2,100 - $1,000 = a profit of $1,100 and you still have your stock at the initial value.

Everyone's risk tolerance is different so if you are the kind of person who wanted to insure your stock in the first place you may not want to keep the stock with no insurance.

LEARNING 2.1 - If you are a conservative investor you may want to lock in the value of your portfolio. The premiums will still impact on the value of your portfolio.

Case Study 2

You own 1,000 shares of a stock ABC which is currently sitting at a market price of $10 per share.

You decide to buy a Put Option at a strike price of $8.00 with a two month expiry date from today. Because the standard contract on the New York stock exchange only covers 100 shares you purchase 10 contracts at $20.00 a contract.

You are still taking some risk but your Options contract costs you only $200.00 + brokerage (so you still have some insurance).

In the next month the stock price falls to $8.00 a share.

Selling the shares

Your stock is now worth $8000, because you insured the stock at $8.00 there is no point exercising the Options but as the stock price has fallen the Put Option has gone up in value and is now worth $700.00. The Options value has increased primarily because there is still a month before the Option expires (hence time decay has not yet fully kicked in).

If you sell the stock now at market value you will get $8,000 (less brokerage). Selling your Option also will give you a further $700 (less brokerage).

By selling the Options at their current value the difference between the relative values are $10,000 (the previous stock price) - $8,000 (the new stock value) + $700 (the current value of the Options) - $200 (your purchase price of the Options) = - $1500.

So your potential loss is $1,500 instead of the $2000 potential loss (from the fall in the stock price).

LEARNING 2.2 - Purchasing Puts at a lower strike price than your shares market value can still provide some insurance whilst reducing your insurance premiums.

LEARNING 2.3 - Purchasing Puts at a lower strike price and selling the shares and the Options early in the life of the Option can reduce your losses (even after the share price falls).

Selling the Put Options

If your view of the stock is that the recent fall in price was a glitch and you expect that the price will recover very soon, you may want to keep the stock and benefit from the increase in the value of your Options.

By selling the Put Options you will no longer have any insurance on your stock but for this example we will assume that you made the correct call.

Because the stock has fallen the value of the Options is now at $700.

By selling the Options at their current value the difference between the relative values are $10,000 (previous stock price) - $8,000 (the new stock value) - $700 (the current value of the Options) + $200 (your purchase price of the Options) = $1,500

So your potential loss is $1,500 instead of the $2,000 potential loss (from the fall in the stock price).

If you are right, and the stock goes back up to $10 a stock, your stock is now worth the original $10,000 but you have gained on the Options trade as you bought the Options for $200 and sold them for $700.

$700 - $200 = a profit of $500 and you still have your stock at the initial $10,000 value.

Everyone's risk tolerance is different so if you are the kind of person who wanted to insure your stock in the first place you may not want to keep the stock with no insurance.

One point to note is that if you are starting to consider your trading in this mindset you are thinking more like an Options trader than someone just trying to protect their stock portfolio.

LEARNING 2.4 - Purchasing Puts at a lower strike price and then encountering temporary falls in your asset price can provide an opportunity to profit from an increase in the value of your insurance.

Recouping your insurance costs with Call Options

Covered Calls

Few people enjoy paying insurance premiums, even though you are trying to protect your capital. If you are going to purchase Put Options as insurance you may want to offset the costs of those Puts by selling Call Options on the same stock.

The term Covered Calls relates to the fact that you are selling a Call Option whilst holding the underlying stock (to cover the Option in case it is exercised).

Whenever someone buys a Call Options contract another person has to sell that same contract (see chapter four on liquidity with regards to Open Interest) and that seller can be you.

Remember that purchasing a Call Option on a stock gives the buyer the Option (but not the obligation) to purchase a set quantity of a stock at a set price until a set date.

By selling a Call Option you are giving someone the Option to purchase your stock at a set price. For this strategy you want to ensure that the strike price of the Call is higher than the current value of the stock's current market value.

Let's look at a case study using the same 1,000 ABC Shares from earlier in this chapter.

Case Study 3

You own 1,000 shares of a stock ABC which is currently sitting at a market price of $10 per share.

You decide to sell a Call Option at a strike price of $11.50 with a two month expiry date from today. Because the standard contract on the New York stock exchange only covers 100 shares you sell 10 contracts at $90.00 a contract.

You receive $900 for the sale of the Options (less brokerage).

Assuming that you also purchased the Put Option in Case study 1 for $1,000:

You have now paid $1,000 and received $900 so in effect you have only paid $100 for two months insurance (again not including brokerage fees).

Dependent on what the market value of the stock is when the Calls are due to expire, that will determine what happens. Let's look at two potential outcomes.

Outcome 1   When the Options are due to expire, ABC Stock is valued at $11.00 a share.
If the stock is valued at $11.00 but the strike price of the Call Options is $11.50 that means that there is no benefit in the Options purchaser exercising that Call Option.

It would make no sense to exercise the Option to purchase the stock at $11.50 a share when they can be purchased for $11.00 in the open market.

The Call Options therefore expire worthless and you still have your stock (which is now worth $11,000) with no further contractual obligations.

Your Put Options also expire worthless as there is no point for you to exercise them for a guaranteed sale price of $10.00 a share when the market value is $11.00 a share.

LEARNING 2.5 – Selling Covered Calls can limit the profits on your stock portfolio. Dependent on the strike price of your Calls they may not get exercised just because the stock price increases in value.

Outcome 2   When the Options are due to expire ABC Stock is valued at $13.00 a share.

If the stock is valued at $13.00 but the strike price of the Call Options is $11.50 that means that there is a benefit in the Options purchaser exercising that Option.

It now makes sense to exercise the Option to purchase the stock at $11.50 a share as the same stock can be sold again for $13.00 in the open market.

The Call Options are exercised and you have to sell the shares for $11,500. You have limited your profits as you had to sell them for $11.50 a share when they were worth $13.00 a share on the open market. You must remember that you have still made a profit on your shares of $1.50 a share from your initial price of $10.00 a share.

Your Put Options again expire worthless as there is no point for you to exercise them for a guaranteed sale price of $10.00 a share when the market value is $13.00 a share (even if you still had the shares).

LEARNING 2.6 – Selling Covered Calls can limit the profit on your stock portfolio but it doesn't have to negate all of your profits.

LEARNING 2.7 – Selling Covered Calls can be a valid way of offsetting the costs of your Put insurance premiums.

Breaking my own insurance rules

On October 26th 2007 I bought 1,000 ZFX (Zinifex) Shares at a total cost of $18,210.60. ZFX was due to go ex-dividend on October 30th.

The dividend was reported as $0.70 a share which meant I was due a total dividend of $700.

Traditionally the price of a stock falls by the same financial amount of the dividend when the stock goes ex-dividend (in this case $0.70 a share). On a majority of occasions the stock recovers to its pre-dividend price quite quickly. This is known as filling the gap and refers to the price gap between the higher and lower stock price.

I decided that as this stock had filled its gap in the previous five years that I would allow the stock to go ex-dividend and then (expecting a quick recovery) pocket the dividend, selling the stock once its price recovered.

LEARNING 2.8 – Don't buy a stock near its ex-dividend date. There is no guarantee that a stock will fill the dividend gap.

I had always professed that I wouldn't physically hold a stock and I definitely wouldn't hold a stock which I couldn't insure with Put Options.

Purchasing Puts around ex-dividend dates creates specific complications. As stocks tend to fall after a dividend this intrinsic value is factored into Put Options so any benefits from the post dividend fall would be offset by the higher cost of the Puts.

LEARNING 2.9 – Don't buy a stock near its ex-dividend date. The cost of Puts for insurance negate the benefits.

One of my main issues was that I had decided to buy stock just before the market crashed.

Stocks usually fill the ex-dividend gap quickly after the ex-dividend date. I was so sure that the ZFX had started its recovery that (even though I still held a 1,000 shares) I bought five ZFX Call contracts for $5,725.00 on November 15th.

Just to confirm that I was mistaken in my presumptions, when I sold the same five contracts on the same day I received only $3,175!

As the previous years had been Bullish I was confident and so I still hadn't bought any Puts as insurance!

LEARNING 2.10 – Having a rule that states that any stock purchased should be insured with Puts and then purchasing a stock without insuring it with Puts (as soon as possible) is dumb!

ZFX turned out to be a very expensive trade.

Unfortunately I had chosen a time to buy stock when the market was going into freefall.

As the stock kept falling I kept watching and when a $16 stock was worth $9 I finally sold.

As the Dividend was only $700 I should have had a stop loss to sell the stock well before the $9 price point.

LEARNING 2.11 – If you don't insure your stock, ensure that you have a stop loss in place.

I had broken three of my own rules:
1. Owning stock
2. Trading a stock near its ex-dividend date
3. Not insuring my stock.

Twelve months earlier my strategy would have been fine as the resources boom was still alive and well but the market is a fluid beast and we must be prepared to evolve as it does.

I was also considering Covered Calls but as the market was falling so fast this would have been a bad strategy.

On January 22nd 2008 I sold the ZFX shares, recouping $8,125 after brokerage.

LEARNING 2.12 – When I break my trading rules I lose money.

NB: Please be aware that the figures in all of the case studies in this book are only for explanation purposes and should not be taken as guarantees of potential profits or losses. Although brokerage costs are not included (for simplification) you must take them into account for your financial planning. Unfortunately the figures in my losing trades are accurate.

Chapter 3   Candlesticks, OHLC Price Bars and
Indicators

If you are going to trade you need to be able to read a basic chart.

Although my initial training involved the use of Open High/Low Close (OHLC) price bars, over the years I switched to Candlesticks.

Depending on the trading /charting software you are using you can usually set the display for either (and have both set to change colours if they are Bullish or Bearish). Most people have their own preferences between the two but as they are both just an interpretation of the same data I wanted to break them down to their components to clarify this.

OHLC Price Bars

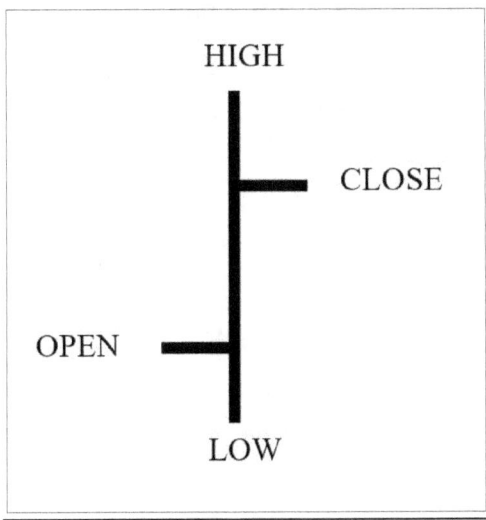

Fig 3.1.   OHLC Price Bar.

The diagram above depicts an OHLC price bar over a specific time period.

For the purposes of simplification we will assume that we are operating on a daily stock chart.

The period of time covered by this bar (and any other bars on this daily chart) equates to one day. The size and shape of this bar would change during the time that the market is open but for this example we will assume that the diagram relates to the data from a previous day and this is the complete data for that day.

The initial horizontal line (on the left of the vertical bar) represents the opening price of the day.

The top of the vertical line is the highest price the stock reached that day and the bottom of the line is the lowest price the stock sunk to that day.

The second horizontal line (on the right of the vertical bar) represents the closing price of the day.

An alternative to OHLC price bars are candlesticks. If you look at Fig 3.1 in comparison to Fig 3.2 & 3.3 below you will see the similarities.

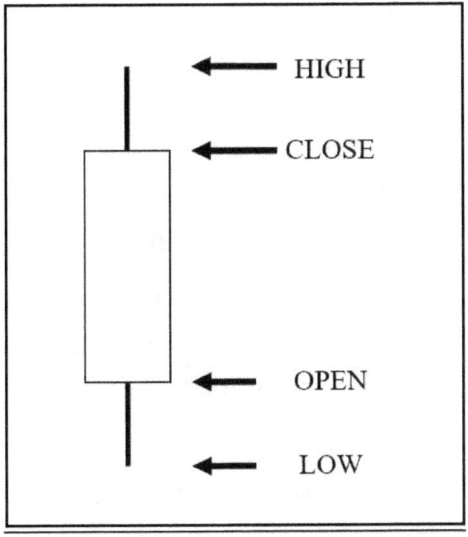

Fig 3.2.   *Candlestick for comparison with OHLC.*

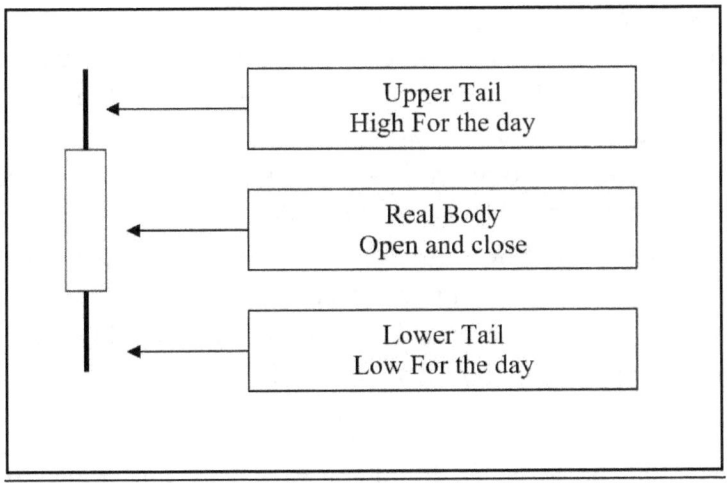

Fig 3.3.   *Simplified Breakdown of a Candlestick.*

Candlestick Indicators

Candlesticks utilise the same information as contained in a Western OHLC Bar Chart, however they look slightly different.

Rather than go into depth with all sorts of patterns that can be formed (Doji's etc.) by the variations of candlesticks I have just included some basic information below to help with a comparison between OHLC and candlesticks.

Although candles can be used for different timeframes I will use the same timeframe of a day for the purposes of simplification.

- The thick part of the candle is also known as the "real body" (this shows the price range between the opening and closing price).
- When the real body is white or empty, the close was higher than the opening price. For simplification coloured charts now show this as a green candle.
- When the real body is black or filled in, the close was lower than the opening price. For simplification coloured charts now show this as a red candle.
- The thin lines above and below the real body are called the wicks, tails or shadows of the candle.
- The upper tail (the high for the day on the daily chart) is located above the Candlestick's body.
- The lower tail (the low for the day on the daily chart) is located below the Candlestick's body.

Just as my trading rules highlight the start and finish of the markets trading day as being volatile periods, the open and close contain the highest levels of significance in candlestick analysis.

The White Candle   -   When the day closes higher than it opened this is a Bullish sign, the price is driven up as the demand outstrips supply.

The Black Candle   -   When the day closes lower than the opening price this is a Bearish sign, the market is pessimistic and supply exceeds demand.

LEARNING 3.1 – Candlesticks are just a different representation of the same data shown on an OHLC price bar.

How I used OHLC

If it is a slow day on a market (i.e. a low volume of trading in comparison with other days) the data the price bar presents may be harder to interpret. One of the factors I took into account in order to ensure the price moves were confirmed was the one third rule.

The one third rule states that the open and close range has to be equivalent to one third of the length of the vertical price range apart. If you apply that to a candlestick (in simple terms) the Real body must be at least a third of the length of the whole candle.

My entry signals confirmations consisted of analysing my chosen stocks (using OHLC charts) to look for the following:

- For Call Options I wanted it to have a Higher High and a Higher Low than the day before.
- For Put Options I wanted it to have a Lower High and a Lower Low than the day before.
- I wanted the Open and Close to be in opposite thirds (dividing the time bar into thirds).

- I wanted the trend to be Bullish for Call Options or Bearish for Put Options
- I drew in all the necessary Support, Resistance and Trend lines and asked myself: Was the Bullish Higher day close to a support line or the Bearish low day close to resistance? (I only proceeded with the trade if the answer was YES)
  NB: Support, Resistance and Trends are covered in depth in chapter 5

How I used Candlesticks

I found the likes of Louise Bedford's "The Secret of Candlestick Charting" very useful but there are lots of books out there if you need to look into candlesticks closer. (Don't be fooled by the title of Bedford's book as candlesticks have been around for thousands of years so they are not really a secret).

Candlestick patterns fall into two broad groups:

1.   Continuation Patterns - The stock will continue over the short-term in a particular direction.

2.   Reversal Pattern - The stock will change direction completely (or simply flatten out into a sideways trend). Reversal patterns are predictive if they occur once a stock is trending.

When all is said and done, trading is partially about using the data presented to try and predict the future based on what has previously happened. Unfortunately the market isn't always logical and in-depth analysis (by minds greater than mine) has shown that candlesticks are only 55% accurate.

LEARNING 3.2 – Candlesticks are only 55% accurate and as such you should use them as confirmation after a move has begun and not as indicators to pre-empt a price move.

Most software out there allows you to view candlesticks, OHLC indicators and more. Whatever indicators or patterns you choose, ensure you don't display so many that they become confusing and make the charts illegible.

As this stage of the book is about providing you a basic grounding in trading I am not going to delve in-depth into the multitude of indicators out there. I initially used Bollinger Bands, RSI, Scholastics and volume, although with Parabolic SAR, Moving Averages, Gant, Volatility, Fibonacci fans and the abundance of other possibilities for charts, it is far too easy to fill a chart up so that the basic information cannot be seen.

As well as indicators, once you start analysing charts you will no doubt start drawing lines between high and low points on your chart and previous high/low points etc.

Drawing too many lines on a chart can present you with the same issue as having too many indicators visible on a chart.

I have mentioned indicators here because the basic price bar (OHLC, Candlestick or other alternative) is the foundation block of your trading. You want to be able to see the price movement on a chart and reduce the white noise.

Imagine any team sport, whether it be rugby, American football, hockey (or any other team sport) and then imagine 100 extra officials (referees, line judges etc.) on the field at the same time as the players. It would be hard to see the players, let alone what was going on with the game.

When you draw too many lines or make too many indicators visible you are creating a similar problem to the excessive officials in the sports analogy above. I know I've laboured this point but it is imperative that you learn to read a basic chart before you obscure it beyond legibility.

LEARNING 3.3 – Whatever Indicators and lines you use on your charts, don't overpopulate the chart.

Chapter 4   Liquidity and Market Makers

Liquidity

Liquidity is your ability to enter a trade and (like any market where products are exchanged) the more buyers and sellers in the market place, the easier it is to enter a trade.

Open Interest is the total number of Options contracts that are not closed or delivered on a particular day. The term "open interest" is also sometimes used to describe the number of buy market orders that exist before the stock market opens.

When I visualize liquidity, I like to think of the old New York Stock Exchange open outcry trading. Prior to digital trading there were large groups of Floor brokers screaming to try and get their trades exercised with other brokers (a hive of activity with lots of liquidity).

One of my early trading rules was never to enter a trade unless an Option had a minimum Open Interest of 150 (see chapter 10 *Trading Rules*).

By having an Open Interest of at least 150, this means that there are at least 150 contracts open in the market (for that specific Option), which provides some semblance of liquidity.

Some people confuse the open interest with the volume but I have provided an explanation below (including the table) to clarify this matter.

When we break things down to basics, the opposite of open is closed.

When someone sells an Option and then buys back that same Option, they have in fact closed out that Option from the market.

When you look at the table below, the volume of Options traded is 12 Options but as Mr Jones has bought back (and closed out) the Option contract that he sold previously, the number of contracts open is only 10.

Day	Buying	Selling	Open Interest	Volume
Trade 1	Mr Smith Buys 1 Options Contract	Mr Jones sells 1 Options Contract	1	1
Trade 2	Mrs Davis Buys 10 Options Contracts	Mrs Frost Buys 10 Options Contracts	11	11
Trade 3	Mr Jones Buys 1 Options Contract	Mr Givens Sells 1 Options Contract	10	12

The liquidity of an Option is very important as there is no point you having an Option that has a value if no one wants to buy it.

True, if you can't sell an Option you can exercise it and make a potential profit that way but Options traders are concerned with leverage and not having to commit the full cost of the stock.

Another one of my initial basic rules was, "Never own more than 20% of the liquidity of an Option".

Never owning more than 20% liquidity in an Option means that if you have to exit a position you have somebody to sell to and you are not in effect trying to trade with yourself.

With advanced strategies such as spreads the 20% liquidity rule may not be strictly adhered to as they are usually placed as a combination order with the market makers.

LEARNING 4.1 – If you enter a trade with limited liquidity you may find it hard to close that trade out (even if your Option has increased in value).

Market Makers

The term "Market Maker" refers to the institutions or companies that create the market to trade in. These companies (traditionally brokerage firms) commit to holding a certain amount of shares, derivatives etc. These companies tend to make their main income from the spread between the Bid and the Ask.

As we have already discussed, it is important to have buyers and sellers in the market.

The Bid and Ask price mean the same in multiple financial markets, so for simplicity we'll just refer to the Options market here.

The Bid price is the price buyers are offering to buy an Option for. If you are selling an Option the Bid is the price that you are offered to sell your Option.

The Ask price is the price that sellers are offering to sell an Option for. If you are buying an Option the Ask is the price that you are offered to buy the Option.

Some companies provide both the Bid and the Ask prices in the market, hoping to make a profit on the spread.

Because these companies provide both Bid and Ask prices, they are in effect making a market for people to trade.

If you find an Option that has no Bid and Ask price displayed, you can usually ask your broker to request a price and this will be displayed for a limited period (provided by a market maker). This is not an issue that most traders will encounter.

One issue when dealing directly with the market makers is that they tend to provide wider spreads, so slippage has more of an impact on your trades than when entering and exiting individual trades.

Slippage is the difference between the expected price of a transaction and the actual price of the transaction.

Case Study

A $24.00 Feb Call Option on ANZ bank has a current market "Bid" of $0.42 whilst the current market "Ask" is $0.54. The mid-point between the Bid and the Ask of the Option is $0.48 and this is the approximate price you would expect the Option to trade at.

Let's assume that you have to buy the Call for $0.50 or sell it for $0.46 (depending on what side of the position you are entering).

The difference between the prices are both the same: $0.50 - $0.48 = $0.02 or $0.48 - $0.46 = $0.02.

In this situation the slippage is therefore $0.02.

In my early trading I gave my broker very little leeway in entering a trade. I might have said buy 10 of the Calls for $0.48 with only 1 cent discretion (meaning he could pay a maximum of $0.49 per contract). Because I was limiting the trade there were occasions where I didn't get into a trade before the price moved.

Once I got a more experienced broker I gave him more room to manoeuvre and surprisingly not only did it cost me very little extra to enter the trades, but he managed to enter more trades for me. If prices are moving fast you do not want to sit on the sidelines of the markets too long.

Nowadays with online trading we tend to place our own trades but the concept is the same.

If you try to buy too cheap (by bidding closer to the Bid price than the Ask price) you may find it hard to enter a trade.

If you try to sell too expensively (by placing your Ask price above the current market Ask price rather than closer to the market Bid price) you may find it hard to enter a trade.

Because you are buying expecting the price to rise, or selling expecting the price to fall, you are not entering a static market. You need to be realistic about the price when you are entering a trade.

LEARNING 4.2 – If you try to buy Options too cheap or sell Options too expensively you may miss out on a profitable trade.

Volatility

Volatility is classed as a measure of the rate and magnitude of the change of prices (up or down) of the underlying stock.

Basically, volatility refers to the amount of risk or uncertainty about the size of changes in a security's value.

I like to think of it as the heartbeat of the market. Low volatility is equivalent to a resting heartbeat and high volatility is a very fast heart rate (pounding).

Volatility is important because it helps to provide momentum in the market. If a stock has a high volatility its price goes up and down more than a stock with low volatility.

The impact on Options premiums is that higher volatility results in higher premiums and lower volatility results in lower premiums.

If you buy an Option on a stock at low volatility and the volatility of the stock increases then even if your stock price rises only a little (or even stays the same) the Option's value may increase. If a bought Option increases in value without the underlying asset increasing in value you can still sell it to experience a profit.

If you sell an Option on a stock at high volatility and the volatility of the stock decreases then even if your stock price falls only a little (or even stays the same) the Option's value may decrease.

If a sold Option decreases in value you may buy it back at a cheaper price than you sold it for and pocket the price difference.

LEARNING 4.3 – When buying Options contracts, aim for low volatility where possible.

LEARNING 4.4 – When selling Options contracts, aim for high volatility where possible.

Chapter 5   Trend Trading

Trends

A trend is defined as "a general direction in which something tends to move" or "the general tendency of a series of data points to move in a certain direction over time".

When a market is trending up (Bullish) it shows that the sentiment of the market is more in favour of buying, which drives the price up due to increased demand. When a market is trending down (Bearish) it shows that the sentiment of the market is more in favour of selling, which drives the price down due to decreased demand.

When tracking the trend of a stock or specific market it is usually monitored as a graph of the price movement against time.

When you look at a line chart (see Fig 5.1) it is usually pretty easy to see the direction of a trend. In order to identify the trend on a bar chart or candlestick chart we tend to draw a line between the candles (see Fig 5.2 & 5.3).

When looking for a Bullish trend we draw a line from the lowest price candle on the chart to the highest price candle on the chart. When looking for a Bearish trend we draw a line from the highest price candle on the chart to the lowest price candle.

Trends tend not to move in a straight line but actually have pauses on their journey. If it went straight up the trading momentum would be short lived so the price trend tends to take dips (retracements) to rebuild momentum.

There's a saying (I quite like) that the route up a mountain isn't a straight line. Just as a mountain climber pauses to catch their breath, a move in a stock price needs to pause to maintain a prolonged move.

As the trend line meanders in a general direction the specific points where it retraces on itself (and then continues in its original direction) form peaks and troughs on a line graph.

On the diagram below (Fig 5.1) the peaks are marked with a "P" and the troughs allocated a "T".

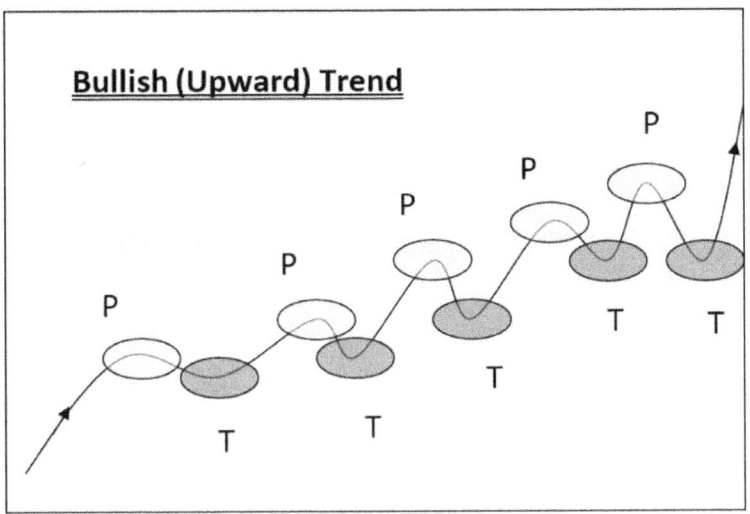

Fig 5.1   Upward Trending Line graph.

A line graph is the most evident visual portrayal of a trend line (see Fig 5.1). It is relatively simple to construct a trend line from other formats of graphs (e.g. Bar charts) by drawing a line joining either the tops or bottoms of the bars together.

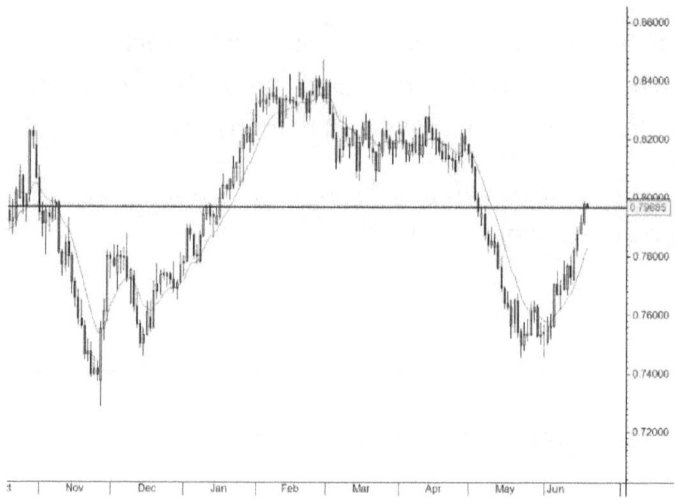

Fig 5.2   *Standard Candlesticks with no Trend line.*

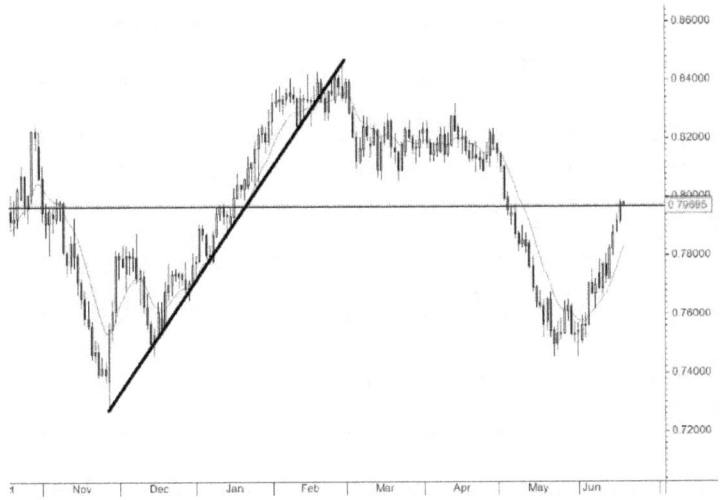

Fig 5.3   *Standard Candlesticks with a Bullish Trend line added.*

In the chart above you can see that there is a Bullish trend on this stock, from mid-November to the end of February. Although the upward trend falters at the end of this period, the price direction is more sideways than down for the next month or so, before it eventually trends down.

When you are following the trend you are said to be trading with the herd as this is the direction that the majority of executed trades are driving the stock price. The thought of following the herd has always conjured up a visual of a cattle stampede for me and if that helps you remember to trade with the trend feel free to use it.

Although some elite traders may trade in front of the herd (in order to attempt to maximize their profits) they risk the chance of calling a trend before it is properly formed. Trends don't last forever but a novice trader may sometimes mistake a retracement for a trend reversal.

During my initial apprenticeship I was advised not to trade against the trend until I had been trading for at least six months.

As it is important to differentiate between a trend change and a retracement, there is a well-recognised criteria for trend confirmation. When I first started trading I adopted this criteria (and have maintained it ever since).

A trend is only confirmed as a trend when it has three higher peaks and three higher troughs (for an upward trend) or three lower peaks and three lower troughs (for a downward trend).

These groups of peaks and troughs must be consecutive or it is not a definitive trend.

If you look at the troughs in the line chart (Fig 5.1) you will see that there are three consecutive higher troughs but the fourth trough is slightly lower.

When I began over-trading (even though I was supposedly limited to the basic strategies), I began to trade the retracements as well as the direction of the trend.

This wasn't because I thought the trend was changing but because I believed I could get in and out of the trades during that retracement.

Because I was trading against the trend (the bulk of the herd) I kept getting trampled.

LEARNING 5.1 – Where possible trade with the trend (the trend is your friend).

Once I started trading the more advanced strategies such as spreads, I learnt ways to benefit from the retracements. Basic strategies of going long on Puts and Calls do not lend themselves to trading retracements and by trying to trade this way early on I took some financial losses.

LEARNING 5.2 – If you are going to attempt to trade retracements, ensure that you are armed with more than just the basic trading strategies.

Trend trading percentages
It was explained to me by my second mentor that out of every ten trades entered, the average trend trader has a 7:2:1 ratio. A 7:2:1 ratio relates to seven losing trades, two break even and one really successful trade. This means that the winning trade needs to be ridden for as long as possible (in order to cover the other nine trades). I shall cover the implications of this ratio more in depth in the money management chapter, *Money Management in Trading*.

Channels

Support

Where a stock price has fallen to a point and then reversed (upwards) this is usually classed as a support area. The support level is the lowest price anyone is willing to sell the stock for.

A support area is an area of a price chart where the price has consolidated below the current stock price. Traders usually join the price bars in the consolidated area with a straight horizontal line below the group of stock prices. If we look at the diagram below we see that a support line has been drawn just above the $0.74 level and is touching the base of three candles. Although we can see a group of candles below the support line earlier in the chart, we now have three points consecutively where the price has failed to breach the low of this support line.

The term "support" relates to the fact that the imaginary boundary is seen as supporting the price (limiting the price from falling any further).

NB: A support line should touch at least three price bars to be classed as relevant.

SUPPORT LINE

Fig 5.4   An identified Support line.

LEARNING 5.3 – For a support line to be valid it should touch the bottom of at least three candles.

Resistance

Where a stock price has risen to a point and then reversed this is usually classed as a resistance area. The resistance level is the highest price anyone is willing to pay for the stock.

A resistance area is an area of a price chart where the price has consolidated above the current stock price. Traders usually join the price bars in the consolidated area with a straight horizontal line above the group of stock prices. (A resistance line as in Fig 5.5). If we look at the diagram below we see that a resistance

61

line has been drawn just above the $0.84 level and is touching the top of at least three candles.

Although one candle has exceeded the resistance line and two end slightly higher than the resistance line we must ensure that the line connects with at least the top of three candles to confirm this resistance level.

The term "resistance" relates to the fact that the imaginary boundary is seen as resisting the price move (limiting the price from rising any further).

NB: *A resistance line should touch at least three price bars to be relevant.*

Fig 5.5   An identified resistance line.

LEARNING 5.4 – For a resistance line to be valid it should touch the top of at least three candles.

Channel

A stock is said to be trading in a channel when it is alternating between a support line and a resistance line. In Fig 5.6 you see a line chart which is a snapshot of a stock price that is oscillating between resistance at around $4 and support at around $2.

Individual traders may vary in how precisely they draw resistance and support lines but the main point to take on board is that when you are trading a channelling stock you are trying to go short when the stock price is starting to fall and go long when the price is beginning to rise.

Because you have identified that the stock is channelling you are looking to buy when the stock price bounces off support and sell when the stock price bounces off resistance.

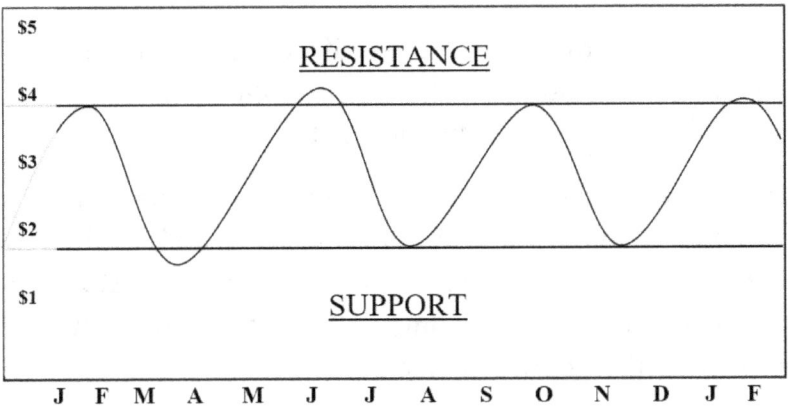

Fig 5.6   A channelling stock identified on a line chart.

The benefits of channels are that they give you previous support and resistance areas to work within.

Trend trading is easier to define than channels as the stock price has a more definitive direction. Within a channel you may be trading against the main trend direction and you have a shorter time frame to enter and exit the trade.

LEARNING 5.5 – Before you trade against the trend study channels.

When I first attempted to trade channels I thought I had it figured out. All I had to do was find a channelling stock and buy Puts on the down swing as the stock price bounced off resistance. Expecting that the price would bounce off the support line I would sell the Puts before they hit support. I'd buy Calls on the upswing as the stock price bounced off support and sell the Calls before they hit resistance.

It's worth noting that what we identify as a channel can just be a point of consolidation. It's also worth noting that a stock price can break out of a channel at any one time.

When trying to trade against the trend I assumed that I had identified a channel. I bought Puts when the stock seemed to be bouncing off a resistance level and then when the stock didn't continue to fall but broke out of the channel (to resume the trend) I looked for patterns that weren't there.

I assumed that the price would resume the fall when it hit the next resistance level but it just kept climbing. I also broke my 20% loss rules because I was so sure that the price would turn again.

The market doesn't care what you believe. If the market doesn't react the way that you expect, you're wrong - not the market.

LEARNING 5.6 – A stock price can break out of a channel at any time.

LEARNING 5.7 – If the market doesn't react the way that you expect, you're wrong – not the market.

LEARNING 5.8 – Stick rigidly to your money management rules, especially when trading against the trend.

SECTION TWO

Chapter 6   The Psychology of a Trader

Analysing charts and determining if a trade meets your entry criteria may seem the backbone of your trading profession. I would suggest that your own personal psychology is the backbone of your trading profession.

The fact that you personally make the decisions when to enter or exit all of your trades can provide immense psychological pressure and this is arguably why most traders fail.

One of the benefits of trading is that you can write your own rules. One of the drawbacks of trading is that you can write your own rules.

In order to be a profitable trader you must adopt the psychology of a successful trader.

Define what or who your support network is
The life of a trader can be a lonely one. Friends, family and colleagues may not know what you are doing. Some may be worried that you are risking your cash and some may be jealous that you are prepared to take a risk and back yourself (see "Plato's Cave" at the end of this chapter).

When you first begin trading you will have enough psychological hurdles to breach so I highly recommend that you choose wisely who you share your journey with. If people enquire how you are doing they are usually just wanting to know how much money you have made. They are not interested in the complexities of trading and if you haven't got large profits to share, their subtle shrugs and comments can subconsciously damage your psyche.

It might seem an advantage to be a loner and not have anyone to pester you about what you are doing. Before you go locking yourself in a dark room with your computer remember there is more to life than trading. Assuming that everyone will be pleased to see you once you hatch from your cocoon (with your trading profits) may result in no one being there.

Ensure that you maintain some social contact when you begin trading. You know those people in your life who will always support you. Because it's hard to explain what you're doing when you are just learning to trade yourself, be selective what you share.

LEARNING 6.1 – Identify your support network for your trading journey.

Gambling or Trading Psychology

In his book "Trading For A Living" Alexander Elder compares traders to the addicts in other support groups (such as Alcoholics Anonymous). Because trading can be a volatile short timescale affair it is possible to become a trading junkie.

You must adhere to your trading rules and that requires mental conviction.

If you are making quick profits it seems easy and you can become a victim of your own success (feeling invincible). If you are making quick losses then just like an addicted gambler you can end up trading more and more often, endeavouring to recoup your losses.

The most important factor to mitigate risk in your trading life is actually you!

If you are trading for the thrill of the trade (like betting on a roulette wheel) then you are gambling not trading.

Although some may look at trading as educated gambling it is crucial that you approach the trading arena as a business and not as a visit to the casino.

Keeping to your written trading rules will help reduce the chance of becoming a gambler and help you become a successful trader.

For years, gurus and mentors have extolled the virtues of trading without emotion.

One of the theories that has been proliferated over the years is that if you are watching a disciplined trader close out a trade you shouldn't be able to tell if they have taken a profit or a loss. Although I have personally only met a few with that perfect disposition, I do believe that reducing the emotion in your trading can make you more successful.

I highly recommend Lenny Levin's book "Emotion Free Trading" (available online as a free pdf) for those interested in practicing more disciplined trading.

Levin's book is a comprehensive guide that has some great techniques for adopting a trader's frame of mind. It's worth noting that no matter how disciplined you believe you are, life has a way of throwing you curved balls.

Don't trade when you have emotional stuff going on in your life – emotion free trading is difficult if you aren't emotion free in your life.

When my marriage broke up I was about $50,000 in the hole but (due to the emotional impacts of the break up) after the split my losses continued if not accelerated.

I tried to convince myself that by throwing myself into trading I was working through my issues (like some kind of therapy). When individuals have huge events in their life there may be some jobs that they can immerse themselves in. Tasks such as data entry may not need much emotional input but owing to the large psychological component of trading you need to constantly remain focused.

LEARNING 6.2 – Take the emotion out of trading. If there are times when you can't detach from your emotions, don't trade.

Knowing yourself
It is essential to work on yourself. Once you know yourself you can create a trading plan that suits you.

For anyone who is aware of the Wealth Dynamics, Myers Briggs (or any other psychometric) profiling systems, you will recognise how diverse profiles react to the same situation differently.

I discovered Wealth Dynamics after I had made my losses and I recognised certain traits in a good trading friend (who has a "Lord" profile) that are not consistent with my "Trader" profile.

As a Lord she is very much concerned with details and that has made her a very successful trader. She lives for back testing and thorough analysis of all her trades and classes herself as a self-confessed geek. I like to do the rapid assessment prior to entering a trade but find the after trade post mortems rather mundane.

Even if you aren't interested in taking a psychometric test you can most likely identify that some of your friends are naturally more detailed, analytic or creative than you.

I am not professing that if you have the wrong profile that you can't make a successful trader. I am acknowledging that knowing your personal attributes will allow you to play to your strengths and determine in which areas you need to focus more of your training.

There are many systems and aptitude tests out there and as well as Roger Hamilton's Wealth Dynamics profile test I do recommend Tom Rath's Strength Finder System.

LEARNING 6.3 – Determine your strengths and which areas of yourself you need to work on.

The term "Paper Trading" relates to the process of mimicking exactly the same actions that you would when live trading but not having any actual funds committed to the trade. Initially this involved just writing the trades down but with modern online trading you can open a virtual account that mirrors the activities of live trading almost exactly. Even in today's digital era it is still referred to as paper trading.

Psychology in relation to virtual trading
The purpose of virtual trading (paper trading) is to practice trading in a safe environment without committing actual cash.

In order to get the maximum benefits from virtual trading you are required to mimic live (cash trading) as closely as possible.

By carrying out the processes in virtual trading exactly as you would with cash it should become second nature and mirror the psychology of cash trading.

It is important to take the paper trading seriously if you intend to trade cash.

My initial mistake was to believe that the emotions of having cash on the table would be different and that I could ignore the losses I had made in paper trading. I wasn't consistently making profits before I switched from paper trading to live trading.

If you are trading online, most brokerage companies will allow you a free virtual account (these tend to be free for 30 days). Different trading platforms/systems tend to have their own idiosyncrasies so I encourage you to thoroughly familiarise yourself with new systems before using them for live cash trading.

When I first started trading I was using a full service broker and placing my trades over the phone.

For my paper trading I used to hold the phone in my hand and pretend to make a call to my broker (working through my script) in order to mimic real trading. I would of course complete my trading logs in exactly the same way as I intended to in my live trading.

My script went something like:

"Hi Robert this is Ged – I'd like to purchase 10 contracts of $24.00 Call Options on ANZ with a Feb 06 expiry. Can you give me the current Bid and Ask of that contract".

"Before I go any further is there any fundamental news that you are aware of on ANZ that may affect the stock price".

Once I'd been trading for a while this became more condensed but I always asked if he knew anything about a stock before I entered a trade (an ex-dividend date could have moved etc.).

For my second bout of trading, technology and virtual accounts allowed me to mirror live trading so closely that I always checked the settings before placing a trade. The switch from my virtual account to my live account was so simple that I only had to click one button and the screens looked identical.

LEARNING 6.4 – You need to be a confident automated virtual trader and transfer the same psychology to cash trading.

LEARNING 6.5 – Ensure that your paper trading is providing consistent profits before switching to live trading.

LEARNING 6.6 – Ensure that you confirm if you are trading your virtual or your live account before placing a trade.

Psychology in live (cash) trading
All things being equal, the psychology in virtual trading should be exactly the same as that for cash trading.

Unfortunately, when people have a cash stake involved (also known as skin in the game) it becomes harder to act.

Although it is difficult to totally take the emotions out of trading, in order to be a successful trader you need to reduce these emotions to a minimum.

The activity of entering or exiting a trade is sometimes referred to as pulling the trigger, for good reason.

Just as the act of pulling a trigger to shoot a weapon involves a psychological decision, committing cash to enter a trade or exiting a trade to take a profit (or realise a loss) requires an emotional decision.

Early profits

When you switch from paper trading to live trading, if your first trades are profitable it can give you a sense of false security. Early profits can make you feel invincible and this can encourage you to take unnecessary risks, such as increasing the percentage of your trading bank per trade.

My first initial live trade was a winning trade with BHP Billiton, where I made a profit of 13% overnight. Unfortunately I was a victim of my own success (although some may think this isn't a large success). Perhaps I would have been more cautious if I had made a loss at first.

While some may suggest that when you are on a roll (a successful series of winning bets) you should continue to gamble at a casino, this does not apply to trading. If you have a set of tested trading rules, the odds that you have two profitable trades in a row are more likely if you search for optimal trades (that meet your rules) rather than trying to extend a winning streak.

LEARNING 6.7 – Don't become over confident if you have a few consecutive winning trades. Emotions cloud your judgement.

Early losses

Just as early profits can affect you psychologically, so can early losses. If you have tested your strategies through paper trading and managed to make consistent profits, you have the potential to make profits in live trading.

If you analysed your paper trading and your profitable strategy produces a ratio of seven losing trades to three winning trades then you should be prepared for a similar ratio when live trading.

Unfortunately the psychology of virtual losses doesn't always transition smoothly to the emotions of real losses. Virtual losses are not as painful as watching your cash being diminished in a live trading bank.

To develop your ratio you may have paper traded several hundred trades and this means that you may have had more than seven losing trades in a row

Even though our previous ratio predicts that we may have seven losses out of ten trades, if your first four trades are losses it can be hard to accept. Early losses can have the effect of making you doubt your strategy and can result in you constantly switching between cash trading and paper trading or just giving up trading.

LEARNING 6.8 – You are going to take some losses in trading so ensure that you know what win/loss ratios to expect.

The pitfalls of intermittent live and paper trading
Working with our seven to three loss to win ratio, if you had four losses in a row (when you first switch to live trading) you may be tempted to switch back to virtual trading.

Assuming that your next three virtual trades are successful you now have to decide if you stay with virtual trading or switch back to live trading.

Even though paper trading is designed to be as close to live trading as possible, it doesn't entail the same emotions and as such you are not trading under the exact same circumstances.

When you switch to live trading you have to accept that you will incur losses and you must maintain the same processes and strategies until you have enough data to determine if your system is profitable.

You must be highly comfortable with virtually trading your system before live trading the same system. If you need to take longer than initially estimated for you to achieve the required comfort levels then invest that extra time. If you can't get comfortable taking virtual losses then do not switch to live trading.

LEARNING 6.9 – Once you are ready to switch to live trading, ensure that you continue to trade until you have sufficient statistics to assess your strategy.

Adding new strategies to your trading arsenal
Once you have been trading profitably for a period of time, you may decide to add new strategies to your trading tool box. I urge caution in being over confident.

I must confess that when I started trading Futures, I assumed that ten years of trading experience meant that I could shortcut parts of the trading system I adopted.

Skills such as being able to read a chart can be transferrable between different strategies but when you are adopting some advanced strategies they may need a different mindset and that can mess with your psyche.

When I first started trading basic Options, the concept of buying at a low price and selling at a higher price wasn't that hard to grasp. Knowing that if the price fell to a set level I needed to exit may not have always been executed but the concept met my instilled understandings.

As I moved on to trading spread strategies that was a whole new ball game. Some spread trades involved me taking long and short positions on the same asset, some spreads involved me selling Options and waiting for them to expire worthless.

When you have developed a basic psychology of:

- Buy (Options) – monitor – Sell (the same Options) = position closed

It is not so simple to switch to a psychology of:

- Buy (Options) – monitor – Sell (different Options on the same asset) – Keep both positions – monitor – maybe close part of the position or maybe let some part of the trade expire worthless.

Or

- Sell (Options) & Buy (different Options on the same asset) –
  monitor – wait for both positions to expire worthless.

Watching Options expire worthless in order to keep the premium that you sold them for can be counterintuitive when you have spent a long time learning that letting an Option expire worthless is one of the deadly sins of Options trading.

I propose not only that you paper trade any new strategy but that you may need to paper trade that new strategy for longer than your previous paper trading (before live trading that strategy).

New strategies can bring new psychological challenges as well as technical challenges so ensuring that you are proficient in both will provide you the best potential for profits.

LEARNING 6.10 – Paper trade any new strategy until you can consistently make profits, bearing in mind that the psychological aspects of a strategy may take more time to adopt than the technical aspects.

Be selective who you share your trading journey with
I feel the need to emphasize this point, as throughout our lives most of us find validation in others' perceptions.

At the start of this chapter I talked about the fact that you may have to contend with detractors who are jealous of your decision to break from the norm. The level of opposition to your choice may vary but I think the "Allegory of the Cave" (written over two thousand years ago) provides a great an insight into individual psychology.

Unfortunately society has conditioned people into a certain way of thinking and I believe that the following paragraphs provide an insight into mental conditioning.

Plato's Allegory of the Cave

Imagine a cave, in which there are three prisoners. The prisoners are tied to some rocks, their arms and legs are bound and their head is tied so that they cannot look at anything but the stone wall in front of them.

These prisoners have been here since birth and have never seen outside of the cave. Behind the prisoners is a fire, and between them is a raised walkway.

People outside the cave walk along this walkway carrying things on their head including: animals, plants, wood and stone.

The Shadows

So, imagine that you are one of the prisoners. You cannot look at anything behind or to the side of you – you must look at the wall in front of you.

When people walk along the walkway, you can see shadows of the objects they are carrying cast on to the wall. If you had never seen the real objects ever before, you would believe that the shadows of objects were 'real'.

The Game
Plato suggests that the prisoners would begin a 'game' of guessing which shadow would appear next. If one of the prisoners were to correctly guess, the others would praise him as clever and say that he were a master of nature.

The Escape
One of the prisoners then escapes from their bindings and leaves the cave. He is shocked at the world he discovers outside the cave and does not believe it can be real.

As he becomes used to his new surroundings, he realizes that his former view of reality was wrong. He begins to understand his new world, and sees that the Sun is the source of life and goes on an intellectual journey where he discovers beauty and meaning.

He sees that his former life, and the guessing game they played is useless.

The Return
The prisoner returns to the cave, to inform the other prisoners of his findings. They do not believe him and threaten to kill him if he tries to set them free.

The crux of Plato's story is that we become so comfortable in our beliefs that when they are questioned we are willing to blindly dismiss others with alternative views. You may be open to new ideas but your friends and family may be so ensconced in their financial beliefs that they openly oppose you.

PROFITABLE STOCK OPTIONS TRADING

Chapter 7   Training and Mentors

Selecting your training, course or mentor

What results do you want to achieve from a training, course or mentor?

If the answer to the question above is just "to make lots of money" you need to take a step back.

If you approach trading as a profession you should realize that like any career path you will require different tools as your competency grows. Individuals approach trading from many backgrounds and capabilities and the onus is on you to do your own self-evaluation.

As humans we are primarily programmed to want certainty so if you are just starting out in trading you may want to trade someone else's system that is already set up.

Your initial training

To give you some feeling of control, your first foray into the trading field may involve you finding a successful trader and adopting their trading methods. If you adopt someone's system or use a set of proprietary indicators (sometimes known as a Black Box) to trade, you must ensure that you undertake some due diligence.

Although some courses and training may provide a money back guarantee on their fees, this will not replace any potential losses that your trading bank incurs.

Just because there are only a small percentage of successful traders out there doesn't mean that you can't be one of them.

The responsibility for your trading success is up to you so choose the training to meet your needs.

Some trading courses are cheaper up front but as they have a caveat of "individual results may vary", you may have further fees for personalized training. You may prefer the immersion of attending a boot camp type training (with a trading guru) or you may choose just to learn from books.

Before you invest too much time or money in initial training, look at what you want it to provide.

If you want a system that just trades automatically (with little time input) then trading may not be the right venture for you. Initially you are going to have to commit a substantial amount of time, as we see in to the other chapters on Time Commitments and Opportunity Costs. Relying on someone else's system may not provide you the freedom that you initially sought. Remember you must consider your budget for your initial education.

My initial structured training

My Initial training involved an intensive three day course that left me with a comprehensive set of notes, a set of audio CDs (of the course) and a group of great friends.

I must compliment the course presenter – who later became a mentor – for the great resources and training.

This was the $4,000 course that I mentioned in the intro to this book and as I suggested, I subscribed to this course with very little due diligence (what some would actually class as reckless abandonment).

LEARNING 7.1 – Always carry out due diligence before committing substantial amounts of cash to your trading education.

It is interesting to note that many people pay out good money for self-development or other courses but do not use what they have learnt. The group that attended the weekend training with me consisted of approximately 50 or 60 people yet after the course only a dozen or so traded for more than a short time. Some of the course attendees never traded at all.

I'm aware that some individuals are "Course Junkies" and seem to just want to pay money for an education that they will never use.

As my initial training had covered basic Long Call and Long Put strategies, this is what I stuck with in the early days of learning my craft.

My first trading arena was the Australian Stock Exchange (ASX) and there were only around 70 to 80 stocks that had exchange traded Options available. Living in New Zealand meant that the time difference gave me the benefits of late starts.

Of the stocks available, I only looked in depth at 20 or so stocks and actually predominantly traded only around a dozen. This list of 20 stocks was known as my watch list.

There are pros and cons in restricting your trading to a small group of stocks

Pros:
- With a smaller group of stocks it is easier to keep a track of the fundamental factors that may influence the stock price.
- Limiting your trades means that you can concentrate on high probability returns and this can reduce your losses.

Cons:
- If you are restricting your trading pool with basic strategies this may limit the quantity of trades that you can find that meet your entry signals.
- Limited trading means limited revenue and if you are trading for a living you may not survive.

After attending the course, the next stage of my training was paper (virtual) trading. Here I carried out the same process of market analysis for entry signals as I intended to continue when cash trading.

Basic entry signal criteria
My initial entry signal confirmations consisted of analysing my chosen stocks (using OHLC charts) to look for the following:

- For Call Options I wanted it to have a Higher High and a Higher Low than the day before.
- For Put Options I wanted it to have a Lower High and a Lower Low than the day before.
- I wanted the open and close to be in opposite thirds (dividing the time bar into thirds).
- I wanted the trend to be a Bullish for Call Options or Bearish for Put Options.

- I drew in all the necessary support, resistance and trend lines and asked myself if the Bullish higher day was close to a support line or the Bearish lower day was close to resistance? (I only proceeded with the trade if the answer was YES).

NB: For more detailed info see my trading rules in chapter 10.

I personally paper traded for two months before I put any money into trading. Unfortunately I made the mistake of not being a (consistent) successful virtual trader before I put skin in the game.

I made myself believe that paper trading was boring and that to get the real experience required to become a successful trader I needed to make those early cash losses that the elite traders make.

Whether or not I was trying to create a self-fulfilling prophecy, I succeeded in transferring my virtual losses into real losses.

LEARNING 7.2 – Ensure that you are trading successfully on paper before you switch to cash trading.

My first cash trade
I have my trading records going back over 12 years; below are the details of my first trade.

January 6th 2005 I bought 4 BHP $15.00 Call Contracts.

Total cost including Brokerage and ACH Fees $1964.08.

January 7th 2005 I sold the 4 BHP $15.00 Call Contracts.

Total returns less Brokerage and ACH Fees $2215.92.

Profit overnight of $251.64 (almost 13%).

My next trade was a 40% loss with the stock "WOW" so potentially I had become a victim of my earlier success.

Trading Logs

When you initially begin to trade, you may have just one position open at a time but as you progress there will be times that you still have one trade open when you enter another.

Remembering that paper (virtual) trading is designed to be as close to cash trading as possible, I ensured that I used the same systems when paper trading as I would in cash trading.

In my early days of trading I found trading logs a good way of keeping a track of the positions I had open as well as ensuring that I took the time to verify that I was trading by my rules. Verification when risking your own money is not a negative.

I used a basic Excel spreadsheet that I completed prior to entering a trade.

My mental arithmetic is pretty good but I ensured some checks and balances by having a few simple formulas in a spreadsheet. The formulas automatically showed me the figures for my potential profit and losses. By taking a little time to input the figures it gave me a few valuable minutes to pause and determine if a trade was actually worth entering.

An example of one of my trading logs

Date	3/01/2008	20% Loss	$0.232	10% Loss	$0.261
Stock	LGL1W	10%Profit	$0.319		
Current Share Price	$3.64	15%Profit	$0.334		
Strike Price	$3.54	20%Profit	$0.348		
Option Type	Call	25%Profit	$0.363		
Expiry Date	Feb-08	30%Profit	$0.377		
Bid	$0.28	Resistance	$3.84		
Ask	$0.33	Move	$0.20		
Buy	$0.29	Delta	0.606		
No Contracts	6.5	Potential Profit $	$0.12		
OI	1946	Potential Profit %	43		
Amount Avail trade	$2,000.00	Amount Per Trade	$307.400		

My Trading Log explained:

Cell	Abbreviation	Explanation
A	Date	The date of entering the trade. This allowed me to review my trades and see not just how long I had been in a trade but back test entry signals during my trading life.
B	Stock	The stock code of the specific Option I was purchasing or selling.
C	Current Share Price	The exact price that the stock had last traded at on the market.
D	Strike Price	The strike price for the specific stock Option I was purchasing or selling.
E	Option Type	This was either a Call or Put (an important factor depending on the market direction).
F	Expiry Date	The Expiry date of the Option (a good check to ensure that the trade doesn't suffer from time decay).
G	Bid	The price that the market is willing to pay for the Option.
H	Ask	The price that the market is willing to sell the Option for.

Cell	Abbreviation	Explanation
I	Buy	Before the trade is placed, this will be the middle of the Bid and Ask to give a rough idea of entry costs. After the trade is entered this is changed to the price paid for the Option to allow exit values to be accurately assessed.
J	No Contracts	The number of contracts that I am purchasing or selling to enter the trade (allows estimation of trade entry costs). This will be rounded down to a whole number.
K	OI	The (Market's) Open Interest in the specific Option.
L	Amount avail trade	The amount of cash available to place in the trade as calculated as a percentage of the trading bank (in relation to the percentages allowed on my trading rules.
M	20% Loss	The value of the Option when it has reached a 20% loss (calculated automatically by the formula).
N	10% Profit	The value of the Option when it has reached a 10% Profit (calculated automatically by the formula).

Cell	Abbreviation	Explanation
O	15% Profit	The value of the Option when it has reached a 15% Profit (calculated automatically by the formula).
P	20% Profit	The value of the Option when it has reached a 20% Profit (calculated automatically by the formula).
Q	25% Profit	The value of the Option when it has reached a 25% Profit (calculated automatically by the formula).
R	30% Profit	The value of the Option when it has reached a 30% Profit (calculated automatically by the formula).
S	Resistance	The next price level (above the current stock price) where the stock price has consolidated. If trading Puts this becomes a support level.
T	Move	The potential movement in price between the current stock price and the price at the estimated resistance level.

Cell	Abbreviation	Explanation
U	Delta	This is the current Delta value of the Option.
V	Potential Profit $	The potential profit as a cash value.
W	Potential Profit %	The potential profit as a percentage of the trade.
X	Amount per trade	The cash amount required to enter a trade. If this figure exceeds the amount of cash available from the trading bank (and that meets the rules) either the number of contracts needs adjusting or the trade is off.
Y	10% Loss	The value of the Option when it has reached a 10% loss

NB if the price of the Bid/Ask/Buy is $0.28 that has to be multiplied by the number of stocks that the Options contract underwrites (e.g.1000) so the actual cost of the trade would be $280 per contract.

Formulas for trading Logs

My trading log is normally in a simple Excel spreadsheet. I have allocated each cell a letter above and duplicated that below to clarify the simple formulas I have completed in each template. I understand that a majority of people can operate a basic spreadsheet. The purpose of the table below is to show that these basic formulas are sufficient to show you the potentials results prior to entering a trade.

Calculation	Cell	Formula	Calculation	Cell	Formula
20% Loss	L	H x 0.8	30% Profit	Q	H x 1.3
10% Profit	M	H x 1.1	Potential Profit $	U	S x T
15% Profit	N	H x 1.15	Potential Profit %	V	U/H x 100
20% Profit	O	H x 1.2	Amount Per Trade	W	H x 1000
25% Profit	P	H x 1.25	10% Loss	X	H x 0.9

Your second level of trading education

When you believe that you are ready for further training you should pursue it.

Before you pursue advanced trading you may want to ensure that you have already attained the level of profit to pay for that training.

The theme of this chapter is constant education but you are the one who needs to evaluate your progress and only you can determine when you are ready to progress to the next trading level.

Logging and reviewing your trades will make it easier to monitor your progress and establish a timetable for the next step in your journey.

My mentoring and advanced (structured) trading

After trading basic strategies for several months I decided that I would have more flexibility in my trading if I could utilize more advanced strategies.

Note that I wasn't making a profit in my basic trading and (rather than a thorough analysis of my basic trading plan) I wrongly determined that it was the lack of opportunities for trades that was restricting my success.

The mentor with whom I had initially trained under had a six month advanced mentoring program which included learning advanced strategies, one-on-one mentoring and direct access to him (so I subscribed).

LEARNING 7.3 – If your basic trading foundation is flawed then making your trades more complex is not a winning formula.

I could now trade basic and more advanced techniques (see chapter 12).

The next stage of my training involved a more intimate group that met once a month and traded live under the mentoring of our initial instructor.

We learnt advanced strategies designed to build on our initial training and also had access to our mentor on a one-to-one basis where required.

I realised that my psychology, wealth and risk profiles were not necessarily the same as my mentor's.

This is no reflection on the skills of my mentor but a further realisation that psychology plays a large part in trading (see chapter 6).

LEARNING 7.4 – Choose your mentor not just on their results but also on their compatibility with your personality and risk profile.

It was during my six months' mentoring that my mentor launched a company that provided a recommended trade service.

The system involved trades being sent out via email and text to tell you when to enter and exit a trade. These trades were chosen for us by our mentor and his team.

What I didn't realize initially was that the way to make money was to trade all of their trades (this became apparent when the company results for the service showed a profit but I did not). Unfortunately with a limited trading bank I wasn't able to trade all of the recommendations.

LEARNING 7.5 – Ensure that your trading bank is large enough to suit any trading system (or service) that you are using.

Unfortunately we all have different risk profiles and unless someone is actually doing the trading for you it is dangerous to have someone lead you into a trade. Entering a trade under someone else's strategy doesn't mean that you can still exit that trade consistent with your trading rules.

The monthly fees for the service retailed around $400 which meant that with a trading bank of $10,000 I needed to make a profit of 4% a month just to cover the fees. When you add my brokerage and the frequent losses, a limited trading bank made the service untenable for me.

The recommendation service I used had no track record which also limited my due diligence.

LEARNING 7.6 – If you choose to use a service that recommends entry and exit points for trades, ensure that you know their track record in detail.

Your ongoing education

Even the best traders in the world are constantly learning and reading in order to enhance their trading. Once you have had your initial training (and potentially intermediate training) and have been profitably trading for a period then you will have a better idea of your progression and the next stage of your education.

My future mentoring and developing my own trading style

After a hiatus of a couple of years away from trading, my return to trading entailed trading Forex (foreign exchange). I realize that this book is for Options traders but the elements of any successful trading system should be adaptable for other markets.

I was drawn to Forex as a friend of mine was having some successes in this field and if the market was working for him it seemed it might also work for me.

Serendipity was working in my favour as I had recently seen a news segment on a locally based man who had just had an Amazon best seller book. The gentleman who had launched the book was someone I had met briefly years previously (at a brokerage launch). Although the book he had launched was a lifestyle book, I remembered that when I first met him he was trading Forex.

Deciding to do due diligence I investigated this trader and found that he was still trading and had several books on trading. After reading his books and further research I found that he sometimes mentored other traders. I approached him and I was fortunate to be enrolled under his mentorship.

Although it might seem that I sought out a local mentor for convenience, I actually searched for a mentor who met a certain criteria (and the location was just a bonus).

I had three main criteria for a mentor:

1.   Someone to allow me to develop my own trading style
By this stage I was aware that my trading psychology and risk profile are not the same as every other trader.

Just because I was looking for a mentor it didn't mean that I wanted to blindly trade somebody else's system.

LEARNING 7.7 – Ensure that any mentor you select fosters your ability to develop your own personal trading system.

2.   A mentor with integrity

Many system providers/gurus out there are interested in upselling you their other products. I am not purporting that they are selling you bad products (as they may believe that their extra products will benefit you) but if they are earning more from their products than their trading it can provide a conflict of interest.

If someone has ultimate belief in their system they may unwittingly steer you towards their system even if that is not the best Option for you.

I wanted someone who I could have the discussion with to determine if we were the best fit for each other. If a mentor is committing his or her valuable time, their actions will show if their priorities are for you to succeed or for them to just add another name to their list.

LEARNING 7.8 – Ensure that your due diligence assesses the integrity of any future mentors.

3.   Someone with a profitable conservative trading history

If we analyze over 90% of the courses and trainers on the market, a majority of them will tout the potential for huge profits.

In most financial investment scenarios the higher the potential returns the higher the risk.

As I had lost over $100,000 in my previous trading ventures I was looking to make profits without wiping out my trading bank.

LEARNING 7.9 – Be aware that with greater potential profits come greater risks and greater potential losses.

Chapter 8   Money Management in Trading

The three most dreaded words in the English language are negative cash flow – David Tang

Trading is a business and you need cash to continue trading. Like any other business, if you run out of cash the business ceases to exist.

Money management is the key to your trading survival. If you switch from paper trading too early a limited trading bank can be wiped out very quickly.

When I first started trading, the mentors around at the time recounted that they had wiped out their first trading banks relatively quickly. Affirming that the intention was for us to learn from their mistakes so we wouldn't have to make our own, they also professed that it was beneficial to make the losses earlier rather than later, as this would reduce the chances of bigger losses further down the track.

I wiped out my first three trading banks relatively quickly and thus assumed I was on the right track.

It is said that only a small number of traders succeed and that a lot of traders give up just before they achieve that success. One reason for giving up is a lack of funds, which is why we need to manage our funds (especially if they are limited).

It is inevitable that you will have some losses but the idea is that you make more on your winning trades than you lose on your losing trades.

This doesn't necessarily mean that you need more winning trades than losing trades. It is the amount of profit from the trades, not the quantity of profitable trades that matter.

Some mentors/advisors recommend splitting your trading bank into 20 equal parts and only placing 5% of your funds on any specific trades. More conservative traders may prefer to limit your individual trades to 2% of your trading bank. This is one way of not putting all your eggs in one basket but a trade with a stake of only $200 can be difficult to make a decent size profit.

The $10,000 Trading Bank
With an initial recommended trading bank of $10,000, my trading rules advised me not to commit more than 20% of my trading bank ($2,000) to any one trade. With a 20% stop loss this meant that in theory I was only committing 4% of my trading bank.

Unfortunately as there are no guaranteed stop losses in Options trading, a large overnight move in the stock price could result in a loss substantially greater than the 20% stop loss.

Only trading high probability trades is another method of money management. This may mean that you spend more time on the side-lines (than you would like) than being in physical trades but remember that basic maths dictates that every loss has to be covered in another trade just to break even on your trading bank.

Some will suggest that you start with as little as $10,000 and some will say you need a much larger trading bank. Whatever the size of your bank, you can lose it just as quickly if you don't maintain money management rules. Money management should be part of your general trading rules.

After wiping out a few $10,000 trading banks over the years, I personally don't recommend starting with such a small trading bank (unless it is sacrificial).

LEARNING 8.1 – A trading bank of $10,000 may be sufficient as your first sacrificial bank (education cost) but it is doubtful that it will provide sufficient returns for your venture to be classed as a business.

Maintaining the allowed percentage for a trade

It can be tempting to exceed your allocated percentage per trade if you begin your trading career with a few losses. Even if you don't intend to change the percentage of your stake it can still have an impact on your balances.

After you initially set the size of the stake that you are going to use per trade, you need to adjust the currency amount as your trading bank balance changes.

If you set a limit of risking 2% of your trading bank per trade your first trade will obviously have a stake of $200. If you set a limit of risking 5% of your trading bank per trade your first trade will obviously have a stake of $500. It might seem easier to keep your initial trades at that same monetary value rather than adjusting this to the percentage value of your trading bank.

I think it's important to look at the potential changes in your capital by basing the trades on monetary value versus percentage value.

Managing your trading balance in regard to losses

Based on a 2% stake, if we look at the table below we can see the difference (in losses) between amending our stake as the balance of our trading bank decreases and keeping it at 2% of our initial trading bank balance.

After only ten trades the difference between our balances is approximately $171 or approximately 1.7% of our initial trading bank.

Although 1.7% may not seem much it is almost the equivalent of the stake for an extra trade when you have only placed ten trades. By reducing the monetary value of our trade as our trading bank declines we can place more numerical trades. As most trading systems are ratio based, every trade counts.

NB: I have omitted any brokerage or trading fees in the examples below for simplicity.

Trade losses based on a 2% stake

Trade No	Monetary Stake	Balance	Adjusted 2% Stake	Balance
1	$200	$9,800	$200	$9,800
2	$200	$9,600	$196	$9,604
3	$200	$9,400	$192	$9,412
4	$200	$9,200	$188	$9,224
5	$200	$9,000	$184	$9,039
6	$200	$8,800	$181	$8,858
7	$200	$8,600	$177	$8,681
8	$200	$8,400	$174	$8,508
9	$200	$8,200	$170	$8,337
10	$200	$8,000	$167	$8,171

Based on a 5% stake if we look at the table below we can see the difference (in our losses) between amending our stake as the balance of our trading bank decreases and keeping it at 5% of our initial trading bank balance.

After only ten trades, the difference between our balances is approximately $987 (almost 10% of our initial trading bank).

By reducing the monetary value of our trade as our trading bank declines we can again place more trades.

Trade losses based on a 5% stake

Trade No	Monetary Stake	Balance	Adjusted 5% Stake	Balance
1	$500	$9,500	$500	$9,500
2	$500	$9,000	$475	$9,025
3	$500	$8,500	$451	$8,574
4	$500	$8,000	$429	$8,145
5	$500	$7,500	$407	$7,738
6	$500	$7,000	$387	$7,351
7	$500	$6,500	$368	$6,983
8	$500	$6,000	$349	$6,634
9	$500	$5,500	$332	$6,302
10	$500	$5,000	$315	$5,987

LEARNING 8.2 – Adjusting the size of your stake in relation to the percentage of your trading bank (as your bank declines) will help reduce your losses.

Managing your trading balance in regard to profits

When we talk about money management we sometimes focus on preserving our capital (understandably, as without capital you can't trade) but we are also referencing profit optimization.

In order to avoid filling this chapter with complex calculations I just want to emphasize the power of adjusting (compounding your profits) with a simple table. For simplicity we will assume that your profit on each trade will be the same as your stake for that trade.

In this example we see that (after only ten trades) the difference in our trading bank balance is over 10% of our initial trading bank.

Trade profits based on a 5% stake

Trade No	Monetary Stake	Balance	Adjusted 5% Stake	Balance
1	$500	$10,500	$500	$10,500
2	$500	$11,000	$525	$11,025
3	$500	$11,500	$551	$11,576
4	$500	$12,000	$579	$12,155
5	$500	$12,500	$608	$12,763
6	$500	$13,000	$638	$13,401
7	$500	$13,500	$670	$14,071
8	$500	$14,000	$704	$14,775
9	$500	$14,500	$739	$15,513
10	$500	$15,000	$776	$16,289

Although later in this chapter I mention a goal of 20% profit, that is an average and for you to achieve that, some of your profitable trades will need to net a lot more than 20%.

The figures in the table above are purely to provide a simplified example but without labouring the facts, I think it is important to note that adjusting your stakes as your trading balance changes can reduce losses and optimize profits.

LEARNING 8.3 – Adjusting the size of your stake in relation to the percentage of your trading bank (as your bank increases) will help optimize profits.

The Warren Buffett factor

There are many courses and gurus out there touting that you can make huge money in trading. I want you to consider Warren Buffett (arguably one of the best traders in the world) and the fact that he produces around 25-35% profits per year.

Let's assume that in your first year you aren't quite Warren Buffett so we'll (generously) assume that you are going to make a 20% profit. Remember this is just an assumption to allow us to perform some projections and for the average trader to make 20% profit in the first year is not standard.

LEARNING 8.4 – If Warren Buffett is only making 35% a year you need to be more conservative in your estimated returns.

Operating costs for a 20% profit

We are going to assume that you are allocating a trading bank of $10,000 solely for trading and this is not to be used for any of your first year's trading expenses.

$10,000 x 20% = $2,000 so you are expecting to make $2,000 profit in your first year. I understand that by adding this to your initial stake you now have $12,000 to trade for your second year (and compounding is a great strategy for growth) but I also want to consider operating costs.

I'm going to imagine that you are wanting to accelerate your trading education so you are going to purchase a course or mentoring program (let's conservatively assume that the initial payment is $4,000).

Cost A = $4,000.

There tend to be ongoing costs for access to mentors, software, indicators etc. (let's conservatively assume that this monthly payment is $150).

Cost B = $1,800 (12months x $150).

I'm going to imagine that you have free access to stationary supplies (I'm not suggesting that you are pilfering from your workplace). As most of us work on iPads or laptops there is less requirement for pens, papers, notebooks etc. You may want to print out the odd chart or your trading rules.

Books are a must and even if you prefer digital to physical books, any successful trader will tell you that you need to read. I have provided a list of recommended books later in this book.

There are lots of cheap kindle books on Amazon (and there is always the library) but you are going to want your own copies of some of the classics like Alexander Elder's books. I am going to conservatively allow you $200 for your initial library.

Cost C = $200.

Total operating costs are $4,000 (Cost A) + $1,800 (Cost B) + $200 (Cost C) = $6,000

- Assuming no trading losses and we are actually making the $2,000, we are actually $4,000 down for the year.

- Operating costs of $6,000 - profits of $2,000 = $4,000 losses.

In order to make our initial $2,000 of estimated profits we now need to make an extra $6,000.

- Initial estimated profits of $2,000 + operating costs of $6,000 = $8,000.

Based on our initial estimates of a 20% profit for our first year we now need a trading bank of $40,000 to achieve this $8,000.

Although $8,000 is 20% of $40,000, because we have had to cover our operating costs we have actually only made $2,000.

- $40,000 x 5% = $2,000 so we only made 5% profit rather than our estimated 20%.

LEARNING 8.5 – When estimating potential profits ensure that you take into account your operating costs.

Topping up your trading bank
Assuming that you have your $10,000 trading bank and you are committing 5% of your bank to each trade then if you had 20 losing trades in a row your trading bank could be wiped out. There are some who would suggest that if you had a larger trading bank (e.g. $50,000) you should only allocate a

percentage of it for your initial trading. If you have $50,000 to trade with and you lose $10,000 as part of your education, you can always start with a new $10,000 bank. If you have only a $10,000 trading bank and no ability to top it up, once it's gone you are out of business.

LEARNING 8.6 – If you have a large trading bank available, don't risk it all when you first start live trading.

Guaranteed stop losses

One of the issues of trading stock Options is that you cannot place guaranteed stop losses. The intrinsic value of an Option is linked to the underlying price value of the stock so if the stock price moves outside of a market's trading hours there is the potential for your actual loss to exceed the level of your stop loss.

A stock such as BHP trades on several international markets so if you purchased BHP Call Options on the NYSE and the price of BHP falls on the ASX, the value of your Options could have fallen more than your stop loss.

I'll use BHP as a case study here to clarify that point:

- Assume I buy 10 Call contracts of BHP at a total cost of $1,000 on the NYSE.
- After the NYSE closes for the night the price of BHP continues to fall on the FTSE and ASX.
- When the NYSE opens up the next day my Options are now worth $400 (down $600).

- If my target was to lose a maximum of $200 (2% of a $10,000 trading bank) I have now tripled that loss. $600 as a percentage of $10,000 is actually 6%.

One of the advantages of trading Forex is that the same market trades around the clock. As there is no down time (market close) during your trading week, your stop losses are more likely to be triggered at your set limits. Forex stop losses are not guaranteed but the added certainty meant that I could leave a position open overnight with limited risk.

When I traded Certificates for Deposit (CFDs) the providers allowed guaranteed stop losses but required a higher premium.

My 20% plus losses
When I initially set out I aimed for a 20% stop loss on a trade but due to overnight moves there were times when a trade lost 60%+.

The way to counteract the potential for overnight losses is to place a trade with a smaller stake. If you intended to risk $200 (20% of a $1,000 trade) then placing a trade for only $200 means that you even if your Option price went to $0.00 you have only lost $200.

Even with a huge overnight price move against you, the guaranteed limit on your losses is 20% of $1,000.

I was restricted because initially I was trading primarily on the ASX which only traded contracts covering 1000 shares. This meant that there would have been very few Options that I could have purchased for less than $500 a contract.

LEARNING 8.7 – If you are trading without a guaranteed stop loss your money management calculations need to factor the potential to lose the whole of your stake in a trade.

The opportunity costs

Although this chapter is entitled "money management" the old adage that "time is money" means that I must address the opportunity costs of trading.

Some people have the money to start the business but are short on time (time poor) and others have the time to start a business but are short on money (money poor).

- If you are "time poor" but have money to invest, the opportunity cost of using your money to invest in Options trading is that you reduce the ability to invest that money in another venture – a venture that could produce a better return on your investment (R.O.I.)
  - o You could be looking at trading as an alternative to your current busy job so you are prepared forgo some other activities (such as sleep) in order to establish your trading business.
  - o If you are just looking at this as an investment for your money but do not have the time for another job on the side, there may be better investments out there for your money (that require less time).

- If you are "money poor" but have the time available to put into Options trading, the opportunity cost of using your time for Options trading is that you reduce the ability to invest that time in another venture to create money. Something as simple as overtime in your current job could provide a better initial financial return on your time investment (R.O.I.) There may be easier/more certain ways to exchange your time for income.
  - o We all have different priorities and someone married with children may prefer to work evenings and

weekends so that they can attend their children's sports events. Someone single and in their early twenties may want to turn that timetable around and so sometimes the same opportunity may not suit both.

o You could invest the time in building another form of online business such as blogging or youtube videos – more time intensive ventures than money intensive and potentially as lucrative.

Returns on investment

One way of managing your money in trading is not to trade at all. In order to allow you to consider if you wish to invest your funds in trading further, I have provided a simplified scenario of the return on investment of $10,000 below.

I am not suggesting that you will find a bank with a guaranteed return of 5% or a hedged fund guaranteeing 10%. We'll use a wage of $10 per hour for ease of calculations. The figures are purely to enable you to appreciate the concepts of other opportunities.

I appreciate that for your trading business I have only allocated you a 20% return on your financial investment yet estimated substantial time for training. This is for your first year, and although long term you may compound that investment, I am giving you a starting point.

Feel free to substitute your own figures in the exercise below.

Simplification of the R.O.I. of a $10,000 investment

A. If you had $10,000 to invest in a bank account with an annual interest for your money of 5% (I won't discuss tax etc.

because everyone has different situations) that's $500 a year for just putting your money in the bank:

- That's an R.O.I. of 5%.
- Little risk.
- No Training Required.
- Little/No Time required to maintain the funds.

B. If you had $10,000 to invest in a managed (hedge) fund with an annual interest for your money of 10% (I won't discuss tax etc. because everyone has different situations) that's $1,000 a year for just putting your money into a hedge fund:

- That's an R.O.I. of 10%.
- A little more risk is involved here as managed funds can result in losses as well as profits but being selective about your fund can reduce risk.
- Some education required (although the sellers of these products will advise you that they are buy and forget, I suggest reading Anthony Robbins "Money Mastery Book" as there can be some hidden costs there).
- Time commitments are still minimal even if you intend to keep an eye on these investments to maintain the level of your funds.

C. If you had $10,000 to invest in Options trading and you could potentially earn $2,000. That's an annual R.O.I for your money of 20% (I won't discuss tax etc. because everyone has different situations) that's $1,500 a year more than the first Option but here you aren't just putting your money in the bank:

- Some risk (potentially your whole $10,000 stake) although you can reduce the amount of risk by taking some of the precautions in this book.
- Quite a bit of training may be required. You may be able to get another $10,000 but you will never get back the hours you invest in any investment opportunity so always think twice before you commit that time (time is money).
- Time required to maintain the funds including:
  - Learning trading strategies, terminology and monitoring the live market.
  - Initially assume 20 hours a week x 52 = 1040 hours.
- The trade-off for those hours:
  - Assuming an hourly rate of $10/hr x 20 hours a week 20 (hours) x 52 (weeks) = $10,400.
  - With your trading business you made the estimated $2,000 profit that's $2,000/ 52 (Weeks)/ 20 (Hours) this gives you a new hourly rate of approx. $1.92 an hour.

Simplistically put, opportunity cost relates to the risk reward returns.
In example 'A' you are taking very little risk with your funds but receiving very little return (and inputting no time) so here the opportunity cost of not receiving extra financial returns is offset by less risk.

In example 'B' you are taking a little more risk with your funds but receiving a bit more return (and inputting some time) so the opportunity cost of not receiving extra financial returns (but receiving more than example A) is offset by a little more risk and some of your valuable time.

In example 'C' you are taking more risk with your funds but receiving more financial return (and inputting substantially more time) so the opportunity cost of using that valuable time to potentially earn more is not offset by the fact that you are earning more R.O.I.

The opportunity cost exercise

In order to help you determine if an Options trading business (or any investment) is for you I have devised a simple exercise below.

N.B. We all have different risk thresholds:
- Some people are happy to risk all of their savings in an investment.
- Some people are only happy to risk 5% of their savings in an investment.

If you have a very low risk threshold then Options trading may not be for you.

Although this calculation isn't exact it can hopefully give a snapshot that can help in your decision making (as per the other disclaimers in this book, please seek professional advice before making any financial investment as this book does not take into account individuals' financial situations).

In order to compare the various costs, certain assumptions are required. If you can get a 10% return from the bank or your hourly rate is $100 feel free to substitute these details into your own calculations.

- For the purpose of comparison we will use an hourly rate of $10/hour.
- We will assume an annual return of 5% on your savings account (all R.O.I.s will be assumed to be annual).

- Although the general estimate for an expert (in any field) is 10,000 hours we will use 1,000 hours as an estimate for competence in a skill you haven't got but need for your business.
- For the purpose of calculations we will use the following values for risk
  - Low risk (conservative investment)
    - 1
  - Medium risk (less conservative investment)
    - 3
  - High risk (building a business)
    - 7
  - Very high risk (using an untested investment strategy)
    - 10

Calculating opportunity costs

You are going to input the details into a table so this exercise can be done via a spreadsheet, MS Word table or even drawing a table with pen and paper.

I.   For any opportunity we will start by completing column **A** with the annual hours we will require to invest in that opportunity.

II.   Now input the amount of cash required to invest in the opportunity into column **B**.

III.   Multiplying the hours (in column **A**) times 10 to give us a dollar value based on our $10/hr wage and input this amount into column **C**.

IV.   Add the monetary value calculated in column **C** to the initial funds required from column **B** to give you the total investment (and input this into column **D**).

V.   Now input your estimated potential yearly revenue for the opportunity in column **E**. We are going to use a ball park figure for the potential return on our investment but before you invest any money in an investment I implore you to crunch the numbers in more detail.

VI.   You need to determine how risky you view the investment (based on your risk tolerance). For these examples we will input the corresponding number from the value we've allocated to each risk category above into column **F**.

VII.   We are now going to calculate the potential to see if the opportunity is worth pursuing.

    a.   Take the figure **E** divide by **D** divide by **F**

    b.   Multiply your answer by **100** and round up to the next whole number.

      c.   The answer to this calculation (your annual R.O.I. %) is written in column **G**

VIII.   Because you are aiming for a high potential return, if you are receiving a low return on your investment, that is stopping you from a greater potential return on the same investment (therefore a low return has a higher opportunity cost).

IX.   The higher the potential figure (in column **G**) the lower the opportunity cost, the lower the figure the higher the opportunity cost.

X.   I have tried to simplify this concept down by providing you data for calculations and worked examples but feel free to work through these calculations a few times if you want.

I appreciate that in a managed fund or bank your funds will compound over time and I realize that you may require less time input in your trading business after the first year but if you believe "time is money" it's worth looking at this for the first year of your investment.

I have provided three examples below of hypothetical data that should hopefully help clarify the process. The examples have been chosen in an attempt to show the comparisons of various risk Options but feel free to run this exercise (by putting your own figures in the blank row) for any investment opportunity you are considering.

Just for fun you may want to input an amount of overtime with your hourly rate (if that's applicable) and see how that compares to the other investment opportunities.

Opportunity	Hours Required ($10/h)	Funds Required	Hours Required x $10 ($)	Total Invested ($)	Potential R.O.I ($)	Risk Factor	Annual %
	A	B	C	D	E	F	G
Savings Account	0	$10,000	$0	$10,000	$500	1	5
Managed Fund	200	$3,000	$2,000	$5,000	$10,000	3	8
Options Trading	1000	$10,000	$10,000	$20,000	$2,000	7	10
Your Opportunity							

Chapter 9   Time Commitments for Trading

Some people approach trading as a part time hobby and some with the intention to substitute their current full time income with a trading income. When I first started trading I was presented with the premise that it was possible to Options trade for a living in only an hour a day.

Companies are still promoting trading for a living in 30 to 60 minutes
Back in 2004 there were several companies advertising and promoting the fact that you can make a substantial amount of money trading for only 30 to 60 minutes a day. In 2017 (as I write this book) there are still companies promoting huge profits from trading binary Options, Forex etc. Today's message of large profits with little time commitment is similar to the messages back in 2004.

Although we would all like to believe that this is all that is required it isn't the full story.

It is my personal opinion that the companies that tout a system purporting that you can make money by trading one hour a day are omitting a few key things.

The time that they are referring to is the time that you are physically entering or exiting trades.

There are systems and tools out there which will enhance your trading and are designed to reduce your time on the markets but like any business venture you need to do your own due diligence.

When I first began trading there were no smart phones. In fact pagers with market tickers were the most used services.

Even with the digital age where we have gone past basic text alerts to instant access to the net via mobile phones and apps, you still need to have your device switched on to monitor the market.

Personally I hate being in a meeting and having someone's mobile interrupting proceedings and if you are trading part time your current employment may not allow you this luxury.

If you intend to trade for a living, remember THIS IS A BUSINESS!

Options trading is a skill that requires training
Options trading (like any other skill) requires training and this will take substantially more than one hour a day.

This is a skill or job and in order to hone that skill you need to monitor the market.

The time that you spend trading will be influenced by factors such as the type of trading, the size of your cash bank, the amount you wish to make, your risk profile etc.

Irrespective of whether you are using fundamental or technical analysis, the chances of reducing the amount of time that you need to spend trading will be dependent on other factors, e.g. how much you already know and how fast you learn.

I realize that there are some individuals out there trading for a short period each day (and making money) but they may have taken several years to get to the stage where they can do that.

Time spent monitoring the market is still counted as trading
Unlike some derivatives, Options do not allow for guaranteed stop losses. If you do not have stop losses and you do not monitor the market outside of your one hour a day you are in danger of making substantial cash losses.

When you are monitoring the market (even if it is through some sort of app or alert service) you are still trading and as such, the one hour a day trading does not stack up.

When individuals promote a business opportunity such as sales or network marketing they may talk about only working ten hours a week for a required income. The work they are referring to is the time sat in front of clients and not all the preparation work and networking that has had to be done behind the scenes to get to those ten hours.

If we presume that the companies suggesting the 60 minute a day timeframe are just not divulging all of the information, they might not be trying to be deliberately deceitful.

LEARNING 9.1 – Your trading time commitment is not just the time spent placing trades.

My time investment
Although my initial training involved DVDs etc. there was no such thing as virtual trading accounts back then. Experience on the markets meant actually sitting in front of a screen and watching the market during live trading hours.

Even though I was only trading on the ASX I have to admit to watching the US markets during the night and wondering what gold and oil were doing.

For my fundamental analysis I was a bit of an addict. Knowing that a hurricane in the Gulf of Mexico would empty the oil platforms and drive the price of oil up meant that I delegated the weather watch to my sister in Florida (a text from someone who was in the path of a hurricane was a bit more relevant to me than an offhand news report).

Technical analysis is also time consuming and one of my shortfalls was not back testing my strategies enough. The historical data was available but I found that part of trading pretty boring. I ensured that I watched the market when it first opened whenever I was in a trade (which was most days).

In Australia there was a 15 minute gap between the share market opening and the Options market opening and this could be painful whenever a stock fell or rose and my Option price went past my 20% stop loss. When the Options market was closed I had no chance to exit the position.

After my first year of trading I had a night job, I was trying to build a business in network marketing and I was also endeavouring to make a living trading.

I treated trading as a business and ensured that I was sat in front of the market for the last hour of each day. With daylight savings times, the Australian / New Zealand time differences and all of my other work, this was sometimes a challenge.

Individuals with children or jobs may find market trading hours don't fit in with their schedules (for trading). When trading, any distraction can be costly so you must be focused. If working from home it may be necessary for you to lock your office door.

LEARNING 9.2 – You must ensure that your timetable and your time slots for trading are synchronized.

During my initial trading there was no dedicated system in New Zealand to provide up to date market data. As I was spending so much time on the markets I started a texting service for a group of my fellow traders and I used to give a 15 minute live update on the main stocks (watch list) we were trading.

LEARNING 9.3 – Whatever time commitment you allocate to trading, you need to be focused when you are physically trading.

Chapter 10   Trading Rules

"I am free, no matter what rules surround me. If I find them tolerable, I tolerate them; if I find them too obnoxious, I break them. I am free because I know that I alone am morally responsible for everything I do."
– Robert A. Heinlein

As a trader you determine your strategies and the framework for your trading.

One of the first things that my initial trading mentor taught me was that if you want to be a successful trader you need to have a set of written rules!

He had a set of rules (which he knew so well that he no longer needed to read them) and he continually said that when he applied his rules he made money and when he broke his rules he lost money.

LEARNING 10.1 – When you apply your trading rules you have a better chance of making money.

The number of rules each trader utilizes can range from a couple to several dozen.

The lists of my trading rules in this chapter are not designed to provide you a standalone trading system but to provide examples of the kind of rules that you may want to use.

Too many rules can cause inaction but I believe that there are some essentials areas that your rules must take into account (listed below in points A-D).

A. When to enter a trade

Whether you are using technical or fundamental analysis to trade, you must have certain criteria for entering a position.

Excessively rigid requirements such as all the stars being aligned prior to entering a trade may be impractical but if you don't have some basic guidelines you may as well be betting on red and black at the casino!

I used to wait until after the Options market had been open for at least a half an hour to let the market settle down from the initial flurries. Having a cooling off period can also allow you better analysis on a price move before placing the trade.

As I was trading the ASX I would usually wait until the last half hour of the market to take a position; this was traditionally when the hedge funds and major players would trade and as they trade larger volumes than the mom and pop traders, they usually influence the direction of a stock.

One of the advantages individual traders have over the large funds/organisations is that an individual can stay on the side-lines for a long period because they don't have to trade (the funds have to trade because that is how they make their money).

LEARNING 10.2 – Ensure that you have met your set criteria before entering a trade.

B. When to exit a trade

Entering a trade can be a lot easier than exiting a trade so you must already have an exit strategy whenever you enter a trade. The strategy must cover when to exit both a winning and a losing trade.

If you are in a losing trade it is easy to believe that the trade will turn around and that you haven't taken a loss until you exit the trade.

Although with advanced strategies it is not always necessary to exit a trade outright (You can convert some strategies into others), you must still have trigger points to indicate when to take action.

If you are in a profitable trade you may decide that there is a lot more profit in the trade but unless you physically take a profit it isn't a profit.

LEARNING 10.3 – Ensure that you already have an exit strategy for any trade before you enter that trade.

C. When to review and amend your rules

As you progress through your trading career, circumstances will change and you must decide when your rules will be reviewed and under what conditions they need to be amended.

An example of a change in circumstances could be several years of a bull market culminating in a big fall followed by a bear market.

Although your strategies should be designed to profit whichever way the market is going, a fundamental change in the world economies may necessitate some adapting of your current rules.

Your trading rules are the guides for your business and just like any business guidelines they need to be reviewed regularly.

If you are sticking rigidly to your rules and are still not getting the results you want, it could be that your rules are wrong.

LEARNING 10.4 – Review your trading rules and their results regularly. Rigidly sticking to your rules but getting bad results could be a fault with your rules.

D. Strategies for different occasions

The phrase "horses for courses" refers to the fact that some horses perform better under certain circumstances. Some horses are better physically suited to running on the flat, some are better at jumping over fences.

Just as there are horses for courses, there are strategies for market direction. Just because you have a set of trading rules and a strategy, it doesn't mean that a specific strategy will suit all markets.

Six market directions

The accepted belief in the trading world is that there are six potential market directions.

The market direction can be applied to the whole market or just to the direction of the asset (asset group) that you are trading.

1. A Bullish Market (moving slowly).

2. A Bullish Market (moving fast).

3. A Sideways Market (moving slowly).

4. A Sideways Market (moving fast).

5. A Bearish Market (moving slowly).

6. A Bearish Market (moving fast).

Although there are six potential market directions you do not need to have a complex trading strategy for every direction. If you are a trend trader you may choose not to trade any sideways markets at all.

On more than one occasion in my trading journey I acted on incomplete information and adopted a strategy that wasn't relevant to the actual direction of the market. There will be times when you are tempted to take a trade before the direction is confirmed (in order to get the maximum potential out of a price move) but if you trade too early you may have the direction wrong.

It is up to you to determine which direction you believe the market is currently moving. Looking at the same chart through different time frames (e.g. an hourly chart, a weekly chart and a monthly chart) can help you confirm if the direction of the move is more corroborated. Specific criteria such as requiring three higher highs and three higher lows to verify a Bullish move can make it easier for you to review your trades later.

LEARNING 10.5 – Ensure that you confirm the direction of the market that you are trading (using set, defined criteria).

LEARNING 10.6 – Ensure that your trading strategy is relevant to the current direction of the market.

My initial trading rules

When I first began trading basic Calls and Puts, I primarily used technical analysis to decide when to exit or enter a trade.

There is a plethora of different indicators that you can have visible on a chart but in the interests of clarity the primary tools I used were Bollinger bands and RSI. I found drawing my own trend lines and support/resistance lines great as it allowed me to only add more elements to a chart when I wanted them visible. I initially used Open High - Low Close price bars as opposed to candlesticks (see Chapter 3).

My initial set of 2004 Options trading rules

Ser	Rule	Remarks
1	Look for a clear break out signal, up or down.	I only traded in that direction.
2	Check the range against the previous day.	Must have met both of these criteria (2a &2b).
2a	For Call Options I want it to have a higher high and a lower low. For Put Options I want it to have a lower high and a lower low.	Calls for up trends and Puts for down trends.
2b	I want the open and close to be in opposite thirds. I want it to be Bullish for Call Options or Bearish for Put Options.	
3	I look at the current trend and observe if the breakout is with the trend or against it.	The trend was my friend.
4	I only trade with the trend until I have traded live for six months (the trend is my friend).	Trading against the trend was not compulsory (even after six months).

Ser	Rule	Remarks
5	I draw in all the necessary support, resistance and trend lines and ask myself:	I adopted "a" or "b" depending which direction I was trading.
5a	Is the Bullish higher day close to a support line? (I only proceed with the trade if the answer is YES).	This helped me determine where to place my stop loss.
5b	Is the Bearish lower day close to a resistance line? (I only proceed with the trade if the answer is YES).	This helped me determine where to place my stop loss.
6	Is the stock in a channel? If so; Is it at the top or the bottom of the channel? I only continue if the Bullish higher day is at the bottom of the channel or a Bearish low day at the top of the channel.	I was looking for confirmation that the channel was continuing.
7	Check if the share price is close to a support, resistance or trend line. I never forget that the trend line may also act as a support or resistance line.	Just because I drew a line on a chart didn't mean that the price would not break through it (but it could act as a barrier).
8	For Call Options I want the share price above the weekly trend line.	I was looking for Bullish breakouts here.
9	For Put Options I want the share price below the weekly trend line.	I was looking for Bearish breakouts here.

Ser	Rule	Remarks
10	If the current share price is outside the Bollinger bands I do not take a new position.	The theory is that Bollingers act like elastic bands and the price can be drawn back into the middle of them.
11	I set profit and loss targets when I enter a trade.	I was aiming for targets of more than 20% but if my view of a trade changed I could exit at 20% or less.
12	I take profits often and tend to sell when my Options reach between 20%-30%	Note I was aiming for profits at a higher level than losses.
13	I sell when my Options reaches 20% losses.	This was for money management.
14	Am I about to "double dip" or attempt to profit twice from the one trading move? I don't "double dip"	If I exited a move previously I obviously expected the move to be stalling or reversing. Entering the same trade again would actually have meant entering a bad trade.
15	I check the last sale price to determine the strike price of my contract	I ensured that the price of the stock matched the strike price of my Option.
16	I pick my Option's strike price, at or in the money	Even a small move in a stock price could add intrinsic value to the Option in this situation.
17	I pick a contract with a minimum of four weeks until expiry. I aim for contracts with six to eight weeks until expiry.	Time decay was my enemy when buying Options.

Ser	Rule	Remarks
18	I check the open interest (O.I.) and only enter the market if the O.I. is a minimum of 150 contracts.	Liquidity was my friend.
19	I stay in a trade no more than seven (trading) days in total.	Avoiding time decay on an Option. If the trade wasn't making a profit I needed to put the funds into a better trade.
20	I never invest more than 20% of my trading bank in any one trade.	Initial money management parameters.
21	I set my loss limit when I trade (20% stop loss is my limit).	Initial money management parameters.
22	I paper trade any strategy for two months before going live.	This was a minimum timeframe.
23	Once live trading, if I have two losing trades in a row I go back to paper trading for two weeks and analyze the two losing trades in detail.	I expected some losses but I needed to ensure that a loss wasn't due to breaking my rules.
24	I buy my trades between 3.00pm and 4.00pm (Sydney time) unless it's the second day of the move.	At the end of the trading day the market had usually determined which direction it was going.

Ser	Rule	Remarks
25	If I don't enter a trade after 3.00pm on the first day of the move, I only enter on the second day of the move (if it is going in the direction of my trend and it fits all of my rules). I then enter between 11.30am and 1.00pm (Sydney Time)	This was in relation to the trading hours on the ASX and was designed to allow me to benefit from a price move if I didn't enter at the start of an acknowledged price move.
26	If I am in a trade and the share price consolidates, I get out of the trade on the third day of consolidation.	Avoiding time decay on an Option.
27	I never buy more than 20% of the liquidity of the total Open Interest.	Initial money management parameters.

These basic rules were compiled to work in conjunction with a basic strategy of buying Calls or Puts and then selling them to exit the trade.

My advanced trading rules

As I progressed to advanced trading strategies, although the basic trading rules remained extant (and were ingrained in me) I adopted some more advanced rules. The more advanced rules also became second nature down the line.

Here is my modified set of Options trading rules from 2005:

Ser	Rule	Remarks
1	Never rush into a trade.	(The extra analysis may cost you a cent or two to enter the trade but may save you a lot more in losses).
2	Always wait for an entry signal before entering a position! Take into account the basic trading rules when carrying out your technical analysis.	I was predominantly building on my basic rules - not ignoring them.
3	Before entering a trade, set profit and loss targets for exiting the position (the exit can be amended and stop losses moved to tie in profits).	In my basic rules these targets would have been 20% but here I was attempting to ride profits.
4	Before entering a trade, review your actions on scenarios.	If the trade went against me shortly after entering the trade I was already prepared to react.
5	Wherever possible, trade with the trend.	The trend was my friend. Follow the herd.
6	Only trade the stocks on my watch list.	(By keeping the watch list to specific stocks I became familiar with them and kept up to date with their fundamentals as well as technical analysis).

Ser	Rule	Remarks
7	Don't enter into a trade before 11.30am Sydney Time.	This time was related to the ASX market opening at 10.00am and meant that I let the market settle before entering a trade.
8	Pick the correct expiry date for your strategy.	Time decay was my enemy for buying strategies and my friend for selling strategies!
9	Try to sell at high volatility and buy at low volatility.	Changes in volatility could benefit me even if there was only a limited price movement.
10	Regularly review your view of the stock.	This applied to technical analysis but fundamentals needed to be monitored the longer I was in a trade.
11	Always know how much available cash you have in your trading bank!	Money management was key to reducing risk.
12	Always know what positions you have open!	This allowed me to continue to spread my risk and correlates with Rule 13.

Ser	Rule	Remarks
13	Don't have your entire trading bank in one sector.	Spreading my bank over different assets reduced risk but if they were all in the same sector I was still open to the same risks (no more than two banks or resources etc.)
14	Check the open interest and only enter the market if the open interest is greater than **150** contracts (unless entering a spread).	Liquidity was my friend for basic purchases. When entering a spread, in order to place all the trades at the same time I had to rely on market makers rather than liquidity.
15	Never invest more than 20% of my bank on any one trade.	In my second bout of trading this percentage was greatly reduced.
16	Always know how much (if any) margin you require.	This was primarily for strategies that involved selling Options.
17	Never buy more than 20% of the liquidity of the total open interest.	In my second bout of trading this percentage was greatly reduced.
18	When you have to exit a strategy just do it!!!!!!!	This was especially important when I was considering switching from a basic to an advanced strategy.

Printed trading rules

There is no point writing a set of trading rules and then ignoring them!

When you initially write your trading rules, keep a printed copy close at hand. Consult your rules before placing a trade (even if this means you only read the whole list of rules at the start of each trading session).

You may believe that you know your trading rules word for word but reading them regularly before placing a trade will reduce the chances of you breaking your rules.

LEARNING 10.7 – Have a written set of trading rules and consult them before entering a trade.

The 5 deadly sins of trading

1. Never let your Options expire worthless. This usually occurs when an Option falls in value and you believe the price is going to recover. By having a stop loss and rigidly closing out the Option you can avoid committing this sin.

2. Never purchase an Option with the wrong strike price. With most online trading platforms it is obvious what the strike price is but if you are just entering a code, double check the strike price before you enter a position.

3. Never purchase an Option with the wrong expiry date. As time decay is your enemy you must ensure that there is enough time left before your Option expires to meet the criteria of your trade.

4. Never buy an Option when you are intending to sell it. With online trading it is becoming easier and easier to place a trade and the ability to take the wrong side of a position is very real.

5. Never sell an Option when you are intending to buy it. With online trading it is becoming easier and easier to place a trade and the ability to take the wrong side of a position is very real.

Chapter 11   Trading Business Plans

I know there may have been some people who rolled their eyes when they saw the words "Business Plan" in the Table of contents but (I know) you are not one of those people.

There are many reasons why people gravitate towards trading and if you have read the section on opportunity costs in chapter 8 (and are still here) you have determined that this is still something you are interested in.

Although some people may trade or buy lottery tickets for fun, the majority of traders want to make a profit. Any serious trader needs to look on this as a business and any successful business needs a plan.

LEARNING 11.1 – If you intend to trade as a business then you need a business plan.

Your business plan will encompass your trading rules, your psychology, money management and many other aspects of the information in the previous chapters.

For a complex business plan you can delve down into the weeds and start looking at strategic profiles (mission statements etc.), internal/ external analysis (Porters Five Forces etc.), competitor profiles (direct and indirect) and so much more.

Unless you want to produce a complex business plan for a funding proposal etc. then the information in this chapter should be sufficient. If you want a more complex business plan you may need to consult a business coach.

As you continue through this chapter you will see that I have laid out a list of some of the points to consider and some of the questions for you to ask yourself to formulate your plans.

By asking yourself these questions and providing your own answers you should start to develop a framework comprising the minimum components that your plan will require.

As well as the eight point framework below, there is also a completed example at the end of this chapter.

A business plan, like any plan is designed to guide your journey from your current position (point A) to a goal destination in the future (point Z).

As well as knowing your destination, you need to know where you are now, what tools you need for the journey and how you are going to monitor the journey. You must know when to correct as you inevitably veer off course.

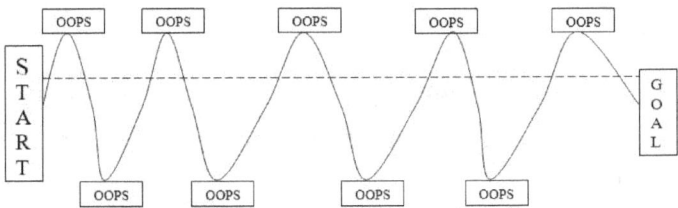

LEARN FROM YOUR MISTAKES BUT DON'T BE AFRAID TO MAKE THEM!

WE SPEND MOST OF THE ROUTE TO OUR GOALS OFF COURSE!

KNOWING WHEN TO CORRECT DETERMINES IF WE WILL ARRIVE AT ALL!

Fig 11.1   *Your business path to your goals.*

LEARNING 11.2 – You need to monitor your business plan as the path to your goals is rarely a straight line.

Components of a trading business plan

When you're determining what components your business plan needs you must initially determine the purpose of your plan. If you reach the stage where you have made a substantial amount of money trading, you may want to provide a prospectus for funding (at which stage you will want a complex/detailed business plan). For most traders just starting out, your plan is primarily a road map to provide direction and monitoring of your trading life.

Your business structure will be different to a traditional retail or services business because you are buying and selling products in an open market.

I have structured a business plan into eight sections below but feel free to add or subtract sections as you see fit:

1. Summary

Traditionally, business plans start with an executive summary. An executive summary, as the title would suggest, summarizes your whole business plan. Traditionally these summaries are one or two pages long. The intention of this chapter is not to produce a huge (100 plus page) business plan. As you may be the only one who gets to read this plan, you may either skip or reduce the size of the summary.

I believe that if the business is just you initially, distilling this down into a mission statement should be sufficient to start with. To help you formulate your mission statement, here are a few questions to consider on what you believe trading will bring you:

- Will trading allow me the opportunity to be my own boss?
- Will trading allow me the opportunity to work as hard as I can to achieve my aims and not promote someone else through my endeavours?
- Will trading allow me the opportunity to generate cash flow that I can invest in other longer term assets?
- Will trading allow me the ability to insure my current stock portfolio?

2. Business description

You might believe that if your business is just you placing the odd trade, that it doesn't need a description. Remember this is a business, not just a hobby, and when it comes to your annual tax return you may want to have this information at hand.

I like the premise that you should be able to explain your business in terms that a small child can understand. This is not diminishing the legitimacy of your business but pointing out that you don't need to over think it.

LEARNING 11.3 – Understanding what your trading business does is one of the basic requirements for running a successful business.

3. Products

In a traditional business plan you would normally detail the goods or services that you traffic with your customers.

In your trading business you will have to determine which financial products suit your requirements.

You can determine which assets/derivatives you are going to trade by confirming if they meet your criteria. I've included a few questions in the comparison below as an example.

a)   An example of an analysis template for a potential product

	Stock Options	Commodities	Forex
Is the market for this product open to trade continuously around the clock?	NO	YES	YES
Can I trade this product in conjunction with my current stock portfolio?	YES	NO	NO
Is the training required to trade this product realistic with the time I have available to learn?	YES	NO	NO

LEARNING 11.4 – Whatever products you are considering trading need to meet your own criteria.

4. Market analysis

In a traditional retail business, you would be analysing the market that you are entering but for trading this is determining which markets or sectors you will trade – what is best suited to your goals.

When evaluating which markets you are going to trade, your current time zone and available hours will predominantly determine your choice.

For basic strategies you may want to trade the DOW or FTSE and stick to a group of around fifteen stocks on your watch list.

For more advanced strategies such as spreads you may look at more volatile stocks but that will depend on the size of your trading bank.

a)   An example of an analysis template for potential markets

	NYSE	ASX	FTSE
What are the market trading hours in relation to the current time zone I live in?			
Are there any clearing house fees (etc.) to trade this market?			
How many Optionable stocks are available to trade on this market?			
What is the average cost of a stock Options contract on this market?			
Do my current work holidays and this market's trading holidays correspond?			

LEARNING 11.5 – Whatever markets you are considering trading need to meet your own criteria.

b)   Market structures

This, simply put, is the cause and effect correlation between various levels of the financial markets.

The diagrams here are primarily to give you an idea of the concept of the top down correlation of components of the financial markets.

Although initially you may only be trading stock Options, I believe it is important to have an overview of where you are in the grand scheme of things, and to understand the way sectors are structured.

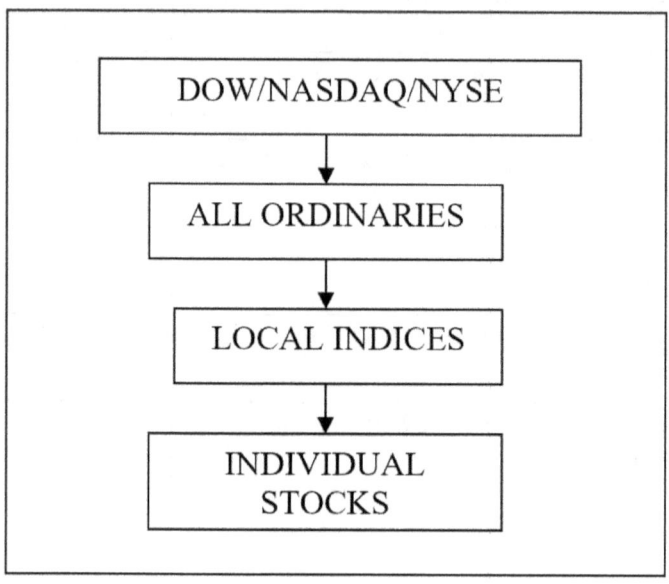

Fig 11.2   *US Markets Top Down Structures.*

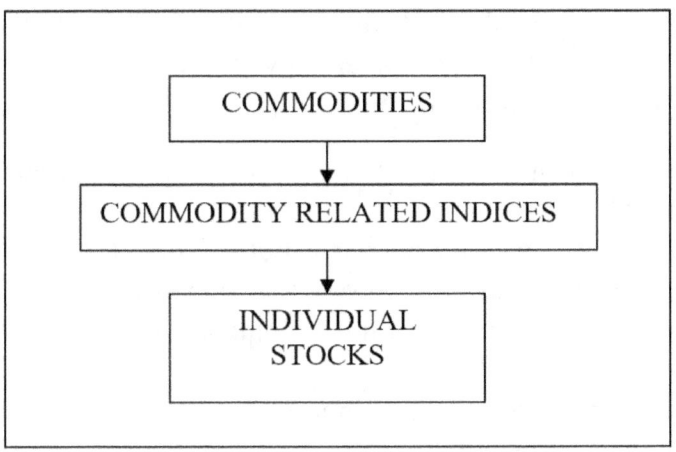

Fig 11.3   *Commodities Top Down Structures.*

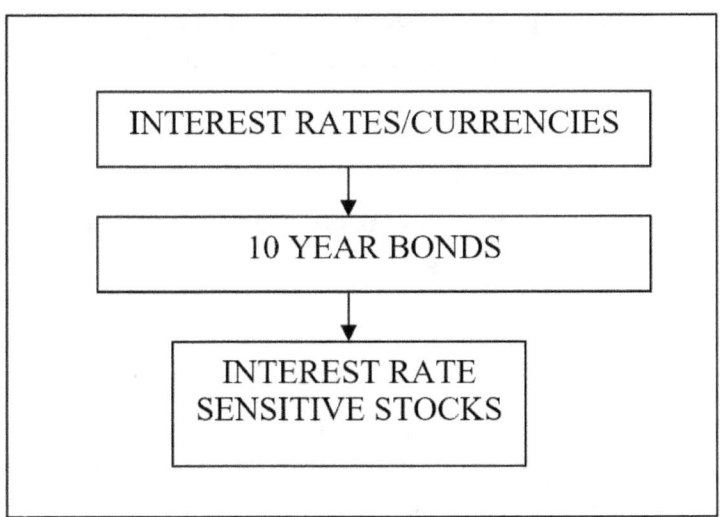

Fig 11.4   *Interest Rates/Currencies Top Down Structures.*

5. Human Resources

Although you may intend to initially carry out all of the functions in this business, like any new employee your business wants to know if you are suitable for the job:

- How long will you paper trade for before switching to live trading?
- Should you provide yourself a bullet point CV and analyse your current strengths, weaknesses, and skill set?
- How do you determine what training or skills you need prior to trading live?
- What is the source and manner of your education (books, training courses or mentors)?
- What are your time commitments (working hours)?
- Dependent on your initial levels of discipline, do you need to work on your psychology?
- Assuming you are trading alone, what is the plan if something happens to you (is there someone who can close out a trade for you if you are incapacitated)?

LEARNING 11.6 – As with any profession, your trading business needs certain competencies.

6. Marketing

In a traditional business plan you would be assessing your marketing to create commerce.

As an individual trader you are not marketing yourself or the financial products you are trading. Your reliance on brokers and service providers to trade requires that you analyze their marketing literature to determine whom you are going to utilize.

Word of mouth referrals tend to be one way that traders initially choose providers but if you don't know any other traders you are going in blind.

I advise you to formulate your criteria into a checklist and use it to compare the various platforms and providers.

a) An example of a simple analysis of three fictional trading sites

	ABC Trading.com	FGH Trading.com	XYZ Brokers4U.net
Does the site provide 24hr support?	Yes	Yes	No
Does the site have the cheapest brokerage fees?	No	Yes	No
Have I had any positive recommendations regarding this site?	Yes	No	Yes
Is the trading platform simple to use?	No	Yes	Yes

LEARNING 11.7 – There are numerous platforms to trade the same financial products so compare them and choose the one that best suits you.

7. Operations

This is the meat of your business and involves the general running activities and systems that will govern your trading business.

- How will you confirm trends (weekly charts)?
- What time frame are you going to trade (hourly/daily charts)?
- Will you bother to observe long term trends as a short term trader?
- What are your specific defined liquidity (open interest) levels to enable you to enter a trade?
- What are your entry signals for the basic strategy?
- What are your trading rules?
- Are you going to leave trades open overnight or close them (to reduce risk)?
- Are you specifically a trend trader or do you also trade channels etc?
- Do you only trade one market?
- What is your plan for transition from paper to live trading?
- How are you going to schedule your trading around vacations or family visits (especially if you have open trades)?
- If you are due to go overseas or away from civilization, how will your trading continue (do you have a rule not to get into a trade two days prior to the trip)?
- What are your milestones to monitor your progress and the requirement for further education?
- Do you have a strategic plan for complex strategies to allow you to react instantly?

8. **Financial Plan.**

Cash flow is king in any business and your trading business is no different.

Before beginning trading it is important that you prepare a financial plan. Below are some recommended contents for your plan:

- A cash flow statement (so that you can understand what your needs are now and will be in the future).
- Profit / revenue projections.
- Your financial goals.
- The size of your initial trading bank.
- The size of your training budget.
- The size of your reserve funds (if you have further funds to risk).
- The percentage of your trading bank that you will commit to each trade.
- The percentage of your trading bank that you will commit to a single sector at any one time (e.g. going Bullish in ten different banks at the same time can be the equivalent of risking ten times your stake in one trade).
- The percentage of your trading bank that you will have committed in the market at any one time (e.g. you may want to never have more than 35% of your trading bank in open trades at once).
- The limits at which you are going to set all of your stop losses and take profits.
- How often you are going to monitor and review your trading finances.
- The timeframe to achieve your financial goals.
- Options to create more capital if your trading bank is wiped out.

LEARNING 11.8 – Cash flow is king in any business and your trading business is no different.

Sample simple business plan

1 Summary
David is a single male aged 52 and his mission is to protect his current stock portfolio of $250,000 worth of Coca Cola Stock for his retirement.

2 Business description
The business is a retirement fund for the end of David's career. It incorporates his current stock portfolio and the use of derivatives to maintain financial growth whilst reducing risk.

3 Products
David will be predominantly buying Coca Cola Puts one strike price below the current Coca Cola stock price and Selling Coca Cola Calls two strike prices above the current Coca Cola stock price.

4 Market analysis
The Options will be traded on the NYSE (as David has already bought his stock on this same market).

5 Human Resources
David already has a basic knowledge of trading Coca Cola stocks (as he has accrued a $250,000 portfolio of Coca Cola shares).

He has determined that Covered Calls are a conservative trading strategy and this is compatible with his risk profile.

Utilizing an online training course (provided by David's broker) he will paper trade for a month before implementing his Covered Calls strategy.

6   Marketing
David's current stock broker provides an online platform that allows him to trade Options.

David will use this platform to trade his Options as whenever his Calls are exercised he gets a discount on brokerage fees.

7   Operations
Thirty minutes is allocated to monitor live trades each Wednesday evening (should access to the online trading not be available on a specific Wednesday this time slot will be adjusted to a new time slot no more than 48 hours away).

Close to Ex Dividend dates no Calls will be sold and the strike price of the bought Puts will be determined by the amount of the dividend. The price of the dividend is usually factored into the price of the Put so buying out-of-the-money Puts is more cost effective (whilst still providing some protection).

8   Financial Plan
The initial price of the stock portfolio has already been paid for ($250,000).

An education fund of $500 has been allocated for the first year (in order for David to fully understand the trading strategies).

An annual dividend of 5% is expected from the stock.

An annual price increase of 10% is estimated for the stock.

The estimated total Options cost is $7,000.

The estimated Annual brokerage fees are $1,250.

Due to certain investment strategies (specific to David) there are no tax implications for the profits from this business.

a)   Cashflow Estimates

	Revenue	Expenses	Balance
Initial Stock Value	$0.00	$0.00	$250,000
Annual Dividend 5%	$12,500	$0.00	$262,500
Stock Price Appreciation 10%	$25,000	$0.00	$287,500
Education Fees	$0.00	$500	$287,000
Estimated Total Options Costs	$0.00	$7,000	$280,000
Estimated Annual Brokerage Fees	$0.00	$1,250	$278,750

b)   Estimated Returns

Initial Value	Annual Value	Annual Revenue	Annual Returns
$250,000	$278,750	$28,750	11%

Chapter 12   Advanced Trading Strategies

During my advanced mentoring sessions I built on my understanding of the basic Long Put and Long Call trades with more advanced strategies.

Over a six month period from March 2005 to August 2005 I added a selection of advanced strategies to my trading toolbox.

Until late 2009 I incorporated these strategies into my everyday trading. Below is a list of some of these strategies:

- Bull Call Spreads.
- Bear Put Spreads.
- Protected Written Calls.
- Protected Written Puts.
- Long Strangles.
- Short Strangles.
- Protected Written Strangles.
- Ratio Put Spreads.
- Ratio Call Spreads.
- Bought Straddles, Reverse Ratio Put Spreads, Synthetic Longs and quite a few more.

Although I became familiar with all of these strategies I didn't need all of them for my everyday trading. In retrospect I could have focused my time on just a limited number of these strategies.

LEARNING 12.1 – Because there are many advanced strategies and combinations of strategies available, be selective which ones you allocate your valuable time to.

It would take me another book to cover all of these strategies in detail. In order to provide sufficient information for an insight into advanced strategies, I will concentrate on just two strategies and the pitfalls therein.

The two strategies we will cover are the Bull Call Spread and Bear Put Spread.

The spread referred to in the title is the gap between two or more strike prices of Options associated with the same underlying asset. (E.g. buying $21 Call Options on Coca Cola and selling $24 Call Options on Coca Cola).

Spreads are usually placed as combination orders. A combination order consists of placing an order to buy a set quantity of Options at the same time as placing another order selling a set quantity of different Options. The orders are placed at the same time and the proviso is that if one order cannot be executed neither of the orders will be executed.

Both the Bull Call Spread and the Bear Put Spread are known as debit spreads.

When entering a spread it falls into one of two categories, a Debit or a Credit Spread.

A Debit Spread
A Debit Spread involves receiving less money from the sold part of the combined strategy than you pay for the bought side of the strategy (when opening a position).

A Credit Spread

A Credit Spread involves receiving more money from the sold part of the combined strategy than you pay for the bought side of the strategy (when opening a position).

Although you receive cash rather than paying cash when entering a Credit Spread, brokers will usually require some equity in case the trade goes against you. This equity can be a set amount of your cash or securities held by the broker.

Combining strategies

I was never very keen on being over exposed with such a small trading bank and as such I tried to avoid Options that I couldn't exit easily.

If you have a basic strategy such as a Long Call and you decide to turn it into a Bull Call Spread (because the stock price has gone down) you are adding brokerage costs to your existing position and limiting your potential to close out of the position.

The premise of advanced strategies is that they not only provide more Options to enter a trade but they also provide the flexibility to switch between strategies already open in order to limit losses (or even to turn a potential loss into a profit).

LEARNING 12.2 – Once you start combining strategies, you are adding costs and dependent on the individual strategy you adopt, you may be just throwing good money after bad.

Bull Call Spreads

As you would expect by the name, a Bull Call Spread is a strategy you use when you have a Bullish view of the stock (you expect the price to rise).

This strategy involves buying a Call Option and writing a Call Option at the same time. You can buy and sell more contracts at the same time but for this strategy the quantities of each must be equal.

For the sold Call Option you will usually pick a strike price at the first or second strike price above the bought Call.

1. The benefits of this strategy
- You can enter trades more cheaply (the sold contracts offset the costs of the bought contracts) where the contracts would otherwise be too expensive for your trading bank.
- The total risk is the total amount paid to enter the trade.
- If the stock falls in price but you expect a rise before the Options expire, you can buy back your sold Options cheaper than you sold them.

2. The drawbacks of this strategy
- Your potential profits are limited to the difference between the strike price of your bought Calls and the strike price of your written Calls.
- If the stock price falls, exiting the strategy outright may not be worthwhile.
- You are paying twice the brokerage of a Long Call Strategy.

3. The factors that determine the strike price which you choose are:

- How far you expect the stock price to rise (estimated by taking into account resistance lines above the current stock price).
- The delta of the bought Option should be approximately double the delta of the sold Options. If the Options don't have this difference in the deltas, a stock price rise will not give the desired effect to the spread (i.e. the bought Options will not increase sufficiently more than the sold Options in value).

An historical Bull Call Spread trade

Below is my trading log for a Bull Call Spread I opened on Lihir Gold in September 2007.

I am not going to provide charts to show my analysis (resistance etc.) as this is an overview and the numbers should speak for themselves.

Stock Price	$3.84	Date	10/09/07			
Expiry	Option	Code	Bid	Ask	Cost	Delta
Nov-07	3.78 Call	LGL1L	0.39	0.42	$0.405	0.586
Nov-07	4.25 Call	LGL6D	0.165	0.21	$0.1875	0.271
Est Cost					$0.2175	
Entry Cost					$0.23	

On September 10th 2007 Lihir Gold was trading at $3.84 a share and I was Bullish the stock.

- LGL1L my $3.78 bought Call was as closest strike price to the $3.84 stock price.
- LGL6D my sold $4.25 Call was the next strike price above the $3.84 stock price.
- The Delta of my bought Call was more than double my sold Call.

Bear Put Spreads

As you would expect by the name, a Bear Put Spread is a strategy you use when you have a Bearish view of the stock (you expect the price to fall).

This is in effect a Bearish mirror of the Bull Call Spread but I will cover all the points for clarity.

This strategy involves buying a Put Option and writing a Put Option at the same time. You can buy and sell more contracts at the same time but the quantities of each must be equal.

For the sold Put Option you will usually pick a strike price at the first or second strike price below the bought Put.

1. The benefits of this strategy
- You can enter trades more cheaply (the sold contracts offset the costs of the bought contracts) where the contracts would otherwise be too expensive for your trading bank.
- The total risk is the total amount paid to enter the trade.

- If the stock rises in price but you expect a fall before the Options expire you can buy back your sold Options cheaper than you sold them.

2. The drawbacks of this strategy
- Your potential profits are limited to the difference between the strike price of your bought Puts and the strike price of your written Puts.
- If the stock price rises, exiting the strategy outright may not be worthwhile.
- You are paying twice the brokerage of a Long Put Strategy.

3. The factors that determine the strike price which you choose are:
- How far you expect the stock price to fall (estimated by taking into account support lines below the current stock price).
- The delta of the bought Option should be approximately double the delta of the sold Options. If the Options don't have this difference in the deltas, a stock price rise will not give the desired effect to the spread (i.e. the bought Options will not increase sufficiently more than the sold Options in value).

LEARNING 12.3 – When entering spread trades, the deltas of the Options are critical.

Strategic Action Plans (SAP)

When we compare a basic trading strategy with a more advanced strategy, we identify that our potential reactions increase significantly.

If you purchase a Call Option and the stock goes up you can sell the Option for a profit.

If you purchase a Call Option and the underlying stock price goes down you can close out the position and sell the Options for a loss.

If you enter a spread position (or turn a basic strategy into a spread) you are presented with more Options if the stock price moves.

Because you need to be able to react decisively when trading, it is critical that you understand your alternatives. If your time slot for trading is limited it is also critical that you are thoroughly conversant with the advanced strategies you intend to trade.

LEARNING 12.4 – If your time slot for trading is limited it is critical that you are thoroughly conversant with the advanced strategies you intend to trade.

One of the ways I prepared to react for stock price moves was to create strategic action plans for each of my trading strategies. In order to determine which actions to take, I think it's important that your SAP includes questions regarding your view of the stock.

Having your SAP ready at hand can ensure that you avoid wasting valuable time (and money).

LEARNING 12.5 – Preparing a strategic action plan for advanced trading strategies will save you critical reaction time.

Below are examples of my initial strategic action plans for Bull Call Spreads and Bear Put Spreads.

N.B. These strategic action plans are presented to show you examples of my thought processes when I was in spread trades and not for you to follow their actions blindly.

Bull Call Spread strategic action plan

Trade	Event	Stock View	Choice	Brokerage	Risks	Margin	Factors	Remarks
Bull Call Spread	Stock price falls to your perceived support level.	Still Bullish	**Buy back the sold Calls turning the position into a Basic Long Call strategy.**	When you entered the strategy you expected two lots of brokerage (in and out). This choice adds no further brokerage.	Your risk is <u>limited</u> to the cost of entering the strategy.	No margin is Incurred.	The point is to buy back the sold Calls for less than they were sold. **Time decay is against you.**	The difference between the sold and the buyback price must take into account brokerage. **Determine why you are still Bullish.**
Bull Call Spread	Stock price falls to your perceived support level.	Still Bullish	**Sell the same amount of Calls as already sold at the same strike price and expiry turning the strategy into a Ratio Call spread.**	Because the sold Calls are the same as the Calls already sold you only have one set of extra brokerage (you still need to take the number of contracts you hold into account for profitability).	Your risk is <u>increased</u> as you now have twice the sold Options that you bought.	If the stock price rises you will be liable for margin.	Delta on sold Calls must not exceed half the delta of the bought Calls. **Time decay is in your favour.**	**Deltas are crucial.** If the stock price falls sharply you must exit the strategy before the strike price of the sold Options is exceeded. If you are wrong and the stock falls you should be able to buy back the sold Options cheaper.

Trade	Event	Stock View	Choice	Brokerage	Risks	Margin	Factors	Remarks
Bull Call Spread	Stock price breaks through your perceived Support level.	Now Bearish	**Sell bought Calls and buy back the sold Calls to take the Loss.**	As with the entry into this position you will have two lots of brokerage on exit.	Your risk is <u>limited</u> to the losses on exiting the strategy.	No margin incurred.	Are there fundamentals (Ex Dividend etc.?).	**Capital preservation is paramount!**
Bull Call Spread	Stock price breaks through your perceived support level.	Now Bearish	**Buy back sold Calls and sell Calls closer to the money turning the strategy into a Protected Written Call.**	If you have to buy back this new position you are now increasing your brokerage so you need to take the number of contracts you hold into account for profitability.	Your risk is <u>increased</u>; If the stock price goes down you will be liable for the difference between the sold and bought strike prices.	This is a credit spread and any premium received may have to be lodged as margin.	Are there fundamentals (Ex Dividend etc.?). **Time decay is in your favour.**	**Why are you now Bearish?** Max profit occurs if the sold Options expire worthless.
Bull Call Spread	Stock price breaks through your perceived support level.	Now Bearish	**Sell the bought Calls leaving the sold Calls naked.**	Because you have not bought back the sold Options currently you have one less lot of brokerage to pay.	Yours risk is <u>increased</u>; If the stock price goes up you have **UNLIMITED LIABILITY.**	Because you are now in a naked strategy you may be liable for a great deal of margin.	**Time decay is in your favour.**	**You must be extremely Bearish to adopt this strategy!**

Bear Put Spread strategic action plan

Trade	Event	Stock View	Choice	Brokerage	Risks	Margin	Factors	Remarks
Bear Put Spread	Stock price rises to your perceived resistance level.	Still Bearish	**Buy back the sold Puts turning the position into a Basic Long Put strategy.**	When you entered the strategy you expected two lots of brokerage (in and out). This choice adds no further brokerage.	Your risk is **limited** to the cost of entering the strategy.	No margin is Incurred.	The point is to buy back the sold Puts for less than they were sold. **Time decay is against you.**	The difference between the sold and the buyback price must take into account brokerage. **Why are you still Bearish?**
Bear Put Spread	Stock price rises to your perceived resistance level.	Still Bearish	**Sell the same amount of Puts as already sold at the same strike price and expiry turning the strategy into a Ratio Put spread.**	Because the sold Puts are the same as the Puts already sold you only have one set of extra brokerage (you still need to take the number of contracts you hold into account for profitability).	Your risk is **increased** as you now have twice the sold Options that you bought.	If the stock price falls you will be liable for margin.	Delta on sold Puts must not exceed half the delta of the bought Puts. **Time decay is in your favour.**	**Deltas are crucial.** If the stock price falls sharply you must exit the strategy before the strike price of the sold Options is exceeded. If you are wrong and the stock rises you should be able to buy back the sold Options cheaper.

Trade	Event	Stock View	Choice	Brokerage	Risks	Margin	Factors	Remarks
Bear Put Spread	Stock price breaks through your perceived resistance level.	Now Bullish	**Sell bought Puts and buy back the sold Puts to take the loss.**	As with the entry into this position you will have two lots of brokerage on exit.	Your risk is **limited** to the losses on exiting the strategy.	No margin is Incurred.	Are there fundamentals (Ex Dividend etc.?).	**Capital preservation is paramount!**
Bear Put Spread	Stock price breaks through your perceived resistance level.	Now Bullish	**Buy back Sold Puts and sell Puts closer to the money turning the strategy into a Protected Written Put.**	If you have to buy back this new position you are now increasing your brokerage so you need to take the number of contracts you hold into account for profitability.	Yours risk is **increased;** If the stock price goes down you will be liable for the difference between the sold and bought strike prices.	This is a credit spread and any premium received may have to be lodged as margin.	Are there fundamentals (Ex Dividend etc.?). **Time decay is in your favour.**	Why are you now Bullish? Max profit occurs if the sold Options expire worthless.
Bear Put Spread	Stock price breaks through your perceived resistance level.	Now Bullish	**Sell the bought Puts leaving the sold Puts naked.**	Because you have not bought back the sold Options currently you have one less lot of brokerage to pay.	Yours risk is **increased;** If the stock price goes down you have **UNLIMITED LIABILITY.**	Because you are now in a naked strategy you may be liable for a great deal of margin.	**Time decay is in your favour.**	**You must be extremely Bullish to adopt this strategy!**

172

Chapter 13   Consolidated Learnings

LEARNING 1.1 – If an underlying asset has a market value less than the strike price of your Call Option (at expiry) there is no point exercising that Call Option.

LEARNING 1.2 – If an underlying asset has a market value more than the strike price of your Put Option (at expiry) there is no point exercising that Put Option.

LEARNING 1.3 – If an underlying asset has a rapid price move, the intrinsic value of the Option can be affected exponentially and rapid action can result in fast profits.

LEARNING 1.4 – If an underlying asset has a limited price move over a set period, the Option will still lose value due to time decay so set a maximum date for holding purchased Options.

LEARNING 2.1 - If you are a conservative investor you may want to lock in the value of your portfolio but the premiums will still impact on the value of your portfolio.

LEARNING 2.2 - Purchasing Puts at a lower strike price than your share's market value can still provide some insurance whilst reducing your insurance premiums.

LEARNING 2.3 - Purchasing Puts at a lower strike price and selling the shares and the Options early in the life of an Option can reduce your losses (after the share price falls).

LEARNING 2.4 - Purchasing Puts at a lower strike price and then encountering temporary falls in your asset price can provide an opportunity to profit from an increase in the value of your insurance.

LEARNING 2.5 – Selling Covered Calls can limit the profits on your stock portfolio. Dependent on the strike price of your Calls they may not get exercised just because the stock price increases in value.

LEARNING 2.6 – Selling Covered Calls can limit the profit on your stock portfolio but it doesn't have to negate all of your profits.

LEARNING 2.7 – Selling Covered Calls can be a valid way of offsetting the costs of your Put insurance premiums.

LEARNING 2.8 – Don't buy a stock near its ex-dividend date. There is no guarantee that a stock will fill the dividend gap.

LEARNING 2.9 – Don't buy a stock near its ex-dividend date. The cost of Puts for insurance negate the benefits.

LEARNING 2.10 – Having a rule that states that any stock purchased should be insured with Puts and purchasing a stock without insuring it with Puts (as soon as possible) is dumb!

LEARNING 2.11 – If you don't insure your stock, ensure that you have a stop loss in place.

LEARNING 2.12 – When I break my trading rules I lose money.

LEARNING 3.1 – Candlesticks are just a different representation of the same data shown on an OHLC price bar.

LEARNING 3.2 – Candlesticks are only 55% accurate and as such you should use them as confirmation after a move has begun and not as indicators to pre-empt a price move.

LEARNING 3.3 – Whatever indicators and lines you use on your charts, don't overpopulate the chart.

LEARNING 4.1 – If you enter a trade with limited liquidity you may find it hard to close that trade out (even if your Option has increased in value).

LEARNING 4.2 – If you try to buy Options too cheap or sell Options too expensively you may miss out on a profitable trade.

LEARNING 4.3 – When buying Options contracts, aim for low volatility where possible.

LEARNING 4.4 – When selling Options contracts, aim for high volatility where possible.

LEARNING 5.1 – Where possible, trade with the trend (the trend is your friend).

LEARNING 5.2 – If you are going to attempt to trade retracements, ensure that you are armed with more than just the basic trading strategies.

LEARNING 5.3 – For a support line to be valid it should touch the bottom of at least three candles.

LEARNING 5.4 – For a resistance line to be valid it should touch the top at least three candles.

LEARNING 5.5 – Before you trade against the trend, study channels.

LEARNING 5.6 – A stock price can break out of a channel at any time.

LEARNING 5.7 – If the market doesn't react the way you expect, you're wrong not the market.

LEARNING 5.8 – Stick rigidly to your money management rules, especially when trading against the trend.

LEARNING 6.1 – Identify your support network for your trading journey.

LEARNING 6.2 – Take the emotion out of trading. If there are times when you can't detach from your emotions, don't trade.

LEARNING 6.3 – Determine your strengths and which areas of yourself you need to work on.

LEARNING 6.4 – You need to be a confident automated virtual trader and transfer the same psychology to cash trading.

LEARNING 6.5 – Ensure that your paper trading is providing consistent profits before switching to live trading.

LEARNING 6.6 – Ensure that you confirm if you are trading your virtual or your live account before placing a trade.

LEARNING 6.7 – Don't become over confident if you have a few consecutive winning trades. Emotions cloud your judgement.

LEARNING 6.8 – You are going to take some losses in trading so ensure that you know what win/loss ratios to expect.

LEARNING 6.9 – Once you are ready to switch to live trading, ensure that you continue to trade until you have sufficient statistics to assess your strategy.

LEARNING 6.10 – Paper trade any new strategy until you can consistently make profits, bearing in mind that the psychological aspects of a strategy may take more time to adopt than the technical aspects.

LEARNING 7.1 – Always carry out due diligence before committing substantial amounts of cash to your trading education.

LEARNING 7.2 – Ensure that you are trading successfully on paper before you switch to cash trading.

LEARNING 7.3 – If your basic trading foundation is flawed then making your trades more complex is not a winning formula.

LEARNING 7.4 – Choose your mentor not just on their results but also on their compatibility with your personality and risk profile.

LEARNING 7.5 – Ensure that your trading bank is large enough to suit any trading system (or service) that you are using.

LEARNING 7.6 – If you choose to use a service that recommends entry and exit points for trades, ensure you know their track record in detail.

LEARNING 7.7 – Ensure that any mentor you select fosters your ability to develop your own personal trading system.

LEARNING 7.8 – Ensure that your due diligence assesses the integrity of any future mentors.

LEARNING 7.9 – Be aware that with greater potential profits come greater risks and greater potential losses.

LEARNING 8.1 – A trading bank of $10,000 may be sufficient as your first sacrificial bank (education cost) but it is doubtful that it will provide sufficient returns for your venture to be classed as a business.

LEARNING 8.2 – Adjusting the size of your stake in relation to the percentage of your trading bank (as your bank declines) will help reduce your losses.

LEARNING 8.3 – Adjusting the size of your stake in relation to the percentage of your trading bank (as your bank increases) will help optimize profits.

LEARNING 8.4 – If Warren Buffett is only making 35% a year you need to be more conservative in your estimated returns.

LEARNING 8.5 – When estimating potential profits, ensure you take into account your operating costs.

LEARNING 8.6 – If you have a large trading bank available, don't risk it all when you first start live trading.

LEARNING 8.7 – If you are trading without a guaranteed stop loss your money management calculations need to factor the potential to lose the whole of your stake in a trade.

LEARNING 9.1 – Your trading time commitment is not just the time spent placing trades.

LEARNING 9.2 – You must ensure that your timetable and your time slots for trading are synchronized.

LEARNING 9.3 – Whatever time commitment you allocate to trading, you need to be focused when you are physically trading.

LEARNING 10.1 – When you apply your trading rules you have a better chance of making money.

LEARNING 10.2 – Ensure that you have met your set criteria before entering a trade.

LEARNING 10.3 – Ensure that you already have an exit strategy for any trade before you enter that trade.

LEARNING 10.4 – Review your trading rules and their results regularly. Rigidly sticking to your rules but getting bad results could be a fault with your rules.

LEARNING 10.5 – Ensure that you confirm the direction of the market that you are trading (using set, defined criteria).

LEARNING 10.6 – Ensure your trading strategy is relevant to the current direction of the market.

LEARNING 10.7 – Have a written set of trading rules and consult them before entering a trade.

LEARNING 11.1 – If you intend to trade as a business then you need a business plan.

LEARNING 11.2 – You need to monitor your business plan as the path to your goals is rarely a straight line.

LEARNING 11.3 – Understanding what your trading business does is one of the basic requirements for running a successful business.

LEARNING 11.4 – Whatever products you are considering trading need to meet your own criteria.

LEARNING 11.5 – Whatever markets you are considering trading need to meet your own criteria.

LEARNING 11.6 – As with any profession, your trading business needs certain competencies.

LEARNING 11.7 – There are numerous platforms to trade the same financial products so compare them and choose the one that best suits you.

LEARNING 11.8 – Cash flow is king in any business and your trading business is no different.

LEARNING 12.1 – Because there are many advanced strategies and combinations of strategies available, be selective which ones you allocate your valuable time to.

LEARNING 12.2 – Once you start combining strategies, you are adding costs, and dependent on the individual strategy you adopt you may be just throwing good money after bad.

LEARNING 12.3 – When entering spread trades, the deltas of the Options are critical.

LEARNING 12.4 – If your time slot for trading is limited, it is critical that you are thoroughly conversant with the advanced strategies you intend to trade.

LEARNING 12.5 – Preparing a strategic action plan for advanced trading strategies will save you critical reaction time.

A

ACH Fees: Australian Clearing House Fees, these are in effect processing fees.

Ask: The price at which someone is willing to sell an Option.

ASX: The abbreviation for the Australian Securities Exchange. A public company that operates Australia's primary securities exchange (allowing trading to take place).

At the money: When the strike price of an Option is equal (or nearly equal) to the market price of the underlying stock.

Australian Clearing House (ACH):   Australian Clearing House Pty Ltd, a wholly owned subsidiary of ASX.

B

Bar Chart: The standard form of chart used in Western Technical analysis.

Bearish: Believing that a particular stock, sector or the overall market is about to fall.

Bear Put spread: Buying one Put Option and selling another Put Option (for the same underlying stock) further out of the money with the same month of expiry. Reduces cost to enter a trade but also limits potential profits.

Bid: The price at which someone is willing to buy an Option.

Black Candle: A Bearish candlestick symbol that demonstrates that the closing price is lower than the opening price.

Brokerage: The fee that you pay to the broker (Online or Full Service) for them to facilitate the trade.

Bullish: Believing that a particular stock, sector or the overall market is about to rise.

Bull Call spread: Buying one Call Option and selling another Call Option (for the same underlying stock) further out of the money with the same month of expiry. This reduces the cost to enter a trade but also limits potential profits.

C

Call Option: A legally binding contract that gives the buyer the Option (but not the obligation) to purchase a set stock at a set price until a set date.

Capital Preservation: Protecting the cash in your trading bank.

CFD (Contract for Difference):   A CFD is a derivative contract between a client and a broker that allows a trader to take advantage of the price movement of an asset without having to own the asset.

Channel: An area on a chart where the price of a stock trades within a set price range over a period of time. The channel limits are defined by a level of support below the trading range and a level of resistance above the trading range.

Close (Closing Price):   The last price that a stock has traded for when the market closes for the day.

Combination orders: Placing an order to buy a set quantity of Options at the same time as placing another order selling a set quantity of different Options. The orders are placed at the same time and the proviso is that if one order cannot be executed, neither of the orders will be executed.

Consolidation: A period of sideways price movement.

Course Junkies: Individuals who continually spend money to attend courses, more as a hobby than with the intention of using the information provided on the course.

Credit Spread: A Spread Options Position in which the price of the Option (or Options) sold is greater than the price of the Option (or Options) bought. You are gaining a profit as you enter the trade.

D

Debit spread: A Spread Options Position in which the price of the Option (or Options) bought is greater than the price of the Option (or Options) sold.

Delta: The rate of change in the Option premium given a change in the stock price.

Derivatives: In the financial markets the term derivative refers to the fact that the value of a product is derived from the value of its underlying asset. With stock Options the price of a stock Option derives from the value of the specific stock that the Options contract relates to.

Dividend: A payment declared by the board (of directors) of a company that is given to its shareholders out of the company's current or retained earnings.

Double Dip: When you enter a trade on the same price movement as you have previously exited it is called double dipping. The theory is that you exited the previous trade because your view of the price direction changed. If a stock price retraces and then confirms another move this is not the same as double dipping as you are now entering another price move.

E

Expiration Date: The day on which an Option expires (ceases to trade) and becomes worthless if not exercised.

Ex-Dividend: The period of time between the announcement of a stock's dividend and the payment of that dividend.

F

Fundamentals: Any factors that could be considered important to the understanding of a particular business (e.g. the gold price could be a fundamental for a gold mine stock).

H

High (Daily): The highest price a stock (or Option) trades at in a day.

I

In the Money: Situation in which an Option's strike price is below the current market price of the stock (for a Call Option) or above the current market price of the stock (for a Put Option).

Index Options: Option based on a stock index such as the S & P 100.

Intrinsic Value: The amount by which an Option is "In the Money". Calculated by taking the difference between the strike price of a stock and the market price of the same stock.

L

Liquidity: The degree of volume traded in a market. The more volume a market trades the more liquid it is.

Long (Long Position): The state of actually owning a commodity or Options contract.

Low (Daily): The lowest price that a stock (or Option) trades at in a day.

M

Margin: The amount of equity required for an investment in stocks or other securities purchased on credit.

Margin Call: A call from your broker to deposit more funds into your trading account. When the amount of funds is insufficient to meet the risk of an open trade the broker wants funds to offset this risk or they will close that trade. A margin call tends to occur when a trade goes against you and is primarily for short positions where you haven't covered that trade with the underlying asset.

Market Makers: Someone who regularly offers a Bid and an Ask price in the market (usually a company or exchange). Individuals who provide liquidity in the market to enable trading to take place.

Market Value: The most recent value that an asset is trading for in the open market.

Mom & Pop Traders: Individual traders who are trading with their own money (not affiliated with a hedge fund or larger companies).

N

Naked (Trading):   An outright short position without related hedge or a spread position. In this case you are selling an Option on a stock (or other asset) without actually owning that stock. Should the trade go against you your potential exposure can be very large.

O

Open Interest: The total number of Options and/or futures contracts that are not closed or delivered on a particular day.

Optionable Stocks: A stock that is classed as an underlying asset that you can trade stock Options on.

Out of the money: When the strike price of a Call Option is higher than the market price of the stock or the strike price of a Put Option is lower than the market price of the stock.

P

Paper (Virtual) trading: The process of mimicking exactly the same actions as you would take when live trading but not having any actual funds committed to the game. Initially this involved just writing the trades down but with modern online trading you can open a virtual account that mirrors the activities of live trading almost exactly. Even in today's digital era it is still referred to as paper trading.

Premium: The amount that the buyer of an Option pays to the seller.

Protected Written Call: Writing a Call Option on an underlying stock at one strike price whilst buying another Call Option on the same stock with a higher strike price. Hence limiting your risk to the spread between the two strike prices.

Protected Written Put: Writing a Put Option (on an underlying stock) at one strike price whilst buying another Put Option on the same stock with a lower strike price. Hence limiting your risk to the spread between the two strike prices.

Put Option: A contract that gives the buyer the Option (but not the obligation) to sell a set stock at a set price until a set date.

R

Ratio Call Spread: An Options strategy in which someone buys a quantity of Call Options and sells a larger quantity of Call Options on the same stock at a higher strike price.

Ratio Put Spread: An Options strategy in which someone buys a quantity of Put Options and sells a larger quantity of Put Options on the same stock at a lower strike price.

Retracement: A reversal in the movement of a stock's price, countering the prevailing trend.

S

Schadenfreude: Someone whose pleasure is derived from the misfortunes of others.

Short (Position):   The state of having sold a commodity or Options contract.

Short Call Options: A stock Option strategy in which an investor sells a Call on a parcel of shares (that are either currently owned or not yet owned).

Skin in the game: Actually having cash invested in the market.

Slippage: The difference between the expected price of a transaction and the actual price of the transaction.

Spread: The difference between the Bid and the Ask of an Option or stock.

Spread Options Position: A trade where you have purchased or sold a number of contracts of Options on the same asset but at different strike prices. The spread is classed as the difference between the different strike prices of the Options.

Stop loss: A stop order placed in relation to a specified price of a stock. When the stop order is triggered by the stock reaching that price, that stock is sold as soon as possible to limit any further losses. When relating a stop loss to a stock Option the order is placed in relation to the price of the stock and triggered in the same way and this results in the Option being sold (or where necessary bought back) to limit any further losses.

Strangle: A strategy where a Call and a Put are either bought or sold at the same time with the same expiry.

Strike price: The specified price on an Option contract at which the contract may be exercised.

T

Technical Analysis: An analysis methodology for forecasting the price movement of a security using historic data of that security. This is primarily done using charts of price and volume information.

Time Decay: The ratio of the change in an Option's price to the decrease in its time to expiration.

V

Volatility: The degree of variability in an asset.

Volume: The number of contracts of an Option sold in one session.

W

Writing an Option: Because Options are legal contracts the act of selling an Option is also referred to as writing an Option.

Like most traders, I have an extensive library of trading books so I have attempted to pare it down to a more manageable list of recommendations for you below

- *A Random Walk Down Wall Street* – Burton G. Malkiel.

- *Adaptive Analysis for Australian Stocks* – Nick Radge.

- *Beating the Street* – Peter Lynch.

- *Conservative Investors Guide to Trading Options* – LeRoy Gross.

- *Even Buffett isn't Perfect* – Vahan Janjigan.

- *Every Day Traders* – Nick Radge.

- *Getting Started in Technical Analysis* – Jack D. Schwager.

- *How I Made Money Using the Nicolas Darvas System, Which Made Him $2,000,000 in the Stock Market* – Steve Burns.

- *Inside the Mind of the Turtles: How the World's Best Traders Master Risk* – Curtis Faith.

- *Liars Poker* – Michael Lewis.

- *Money Mastery the Game* – Anthony Robbins.

- *Options* – Guy Bower.

- *One up on Wall Street* – Peter Lynch.

- *Prophecy* – Robert Kyosaki.

- *Reminiscences of a Stock Operator* – Jesse Livermore.

- *Stock Options* – Robert R. Pastore.

- *Strengths Finder 2.0* – Tom Rath.

- *Super Trader* – Van Tharp.

- *Technical Analysis for Dummies* – Barbara Rockerfeller.

- *The 21 Irrefutable Truths of Trading* – John H. Hayden.

- *The Complete Turtle Trader* – Michael W. Covel.

- *The Intelligent Investor* – Benjamin Graham.

- *The New Market Wizards* – Jack Schwager.

- *The Tao of Warren Buffett* – Mary Buffet & David Clark.

- *The Secret of Candlestick Charting* – Louise Bedford.

- *The Secrets of Emotion Free Trading* – Larry Levin.

- *Trading for a Living* – Dr Alexander Elder.

- *Trading for a Profit* – Oli Hille.

- *Trade Your Way to Financial Freedom* – Van Tharp.

- *Trend Trading* – Daryl Guppy.

- *Wall Street Words* – David L Scott.

- *Warrior Trading* – Clifford Bennet.

- *Winning in the Options Market* – Alan S. Lyons.

- *Your Life Your Legacy* – Roger Hamilton.

Ged's other book:

- *FBA - Building an Amazon Business - The Beginner's Guide: Why and How to Build a Profitable Business on Amazon* – Ged Cusack